THE CIVIL WAR IN KANSAS

THE
CIVIL WAR
— IN —
KANSAS

Ten Years of Turmoil

DEBRA GOODRICH BISEL

Foreword by General Richard B. Myers (USAF, ret.),
15th Chairman of the Joint Chiefs of Staff

THE
History
PRESS

Published by The History Press
Charleston, SC 29403
www.historypress.net

Back cover image of cannon courtesy of Michelle M. Martin/Discovering History.

First published 2012
Second printing 2013

Manufactured in the United States

ISBN 978.1.60949.563.3

Library of Congress Cataloging-in-Publication Data

Bisel, Debra Goodrich.
The Civil War in Kansas : ten years of turmoil / Debra Goodrich Bisel.
pages cm
Includes bibliographical references and index.
ISBN 978-1-60949-563-3
1. Kansas--History--Civil War, 1861-1865. I. Title.
E508.B58 2012
978.1'031--dc23
2012007706

For the Kansans who persevered and sacrificed and hoped for the thirty-fourth star.

For our grandchildren—Laurel, Devyn-Ray, Rylan, Nathaniel and Joshua. Never forget that you are brave and resourceful Kansans.

For my husband, Gary, the best and most talented Kansan I have ever known.

Contents

CONTENTS

Foreword

When you think of Kansas today and those Kansans who helped shaped America, many will think of Dwight D. Eisenhower, a Kansan who left Abilene to become the supreme Allied commander in World War II, oversaw the planning and execution of the Allied invasion of Europe and then became the thirty-fifth president of the United States. As you'll learn in *The Civil War in Kansas: Ten Years of Turmoil*, you have to go further back to find those Kansans, ordinary Kansans, who arguably had the most profound impact on modern America. Most of them are certainly not as well known as President Eisenhower; nevertheless, their courage to follow and act on their beliefs had a remarkable impact on our young country.

In fact, these people started making their voices heard before Kansas became a state. In this book, Debbie Bisel takes us back to the nineteenth century to 1854 and to those years before and during the American Civil War. This contest was a watershed event for the country, and Kansas was at the forefront of this painful period in our nation's history. Events of that period were intricate and complex. If you like reading about political intrigue, terrorism, guerrilla warfare, corruption and stories of great personal sacrifice and courage, you'll be absolutely fascinated by this book. This period not only shaped the state of Kansas but also had a significant impact on America and how it would deal with the subject of slavery.

The Kansas Territory was in the center of the fight by abolitionists and proslavers alike. Nothing is more important than how a country decides to treat its citizens, and this book lays out the debate, passionate on both sides, and gives us insights into those who made history and impacted our country's future. As the author says, "The opening of the Kansas Territory was a glimmer of hope that one day soon a generation of black people could be born free." As this book illuminates, I think you'll be proud of how Kansas pioneers dealt with the most important issue of the times more than 150 years ago.

There continues to be much discussion over exactly what role Kansas did play in our civil war. According to Professor William D. Young at Maple Woods Community College in Kansas City, Missouri, historians come to no consensus on how to examine Kansas's contributions during the Civil War. Questions without definitive answers from historians include whether "Bleeding Kansas" caused the Civil War, when the Civil War actually began in the West and what the actual military importance of Kansas was during the war. One thing is clear, however; no other state's history is so intertwined with the most defining and disruptive event in United States history as Kansas.

In this book, Bisel helps answer the questions that so many other historians debate. When you're finished reading this excellent work, you will have an extraordinary view of events of the period. As you understand them more clearly, you'll be able to form your own opinions on the question of Kansas's contributions before and during our civil war.

This is not your usual history book. If this were a work of fiction, the reader would be spellbound and wonder where the author got such an imagination. But the events and people are real. Bisel makes the history come to life by using the personal experiences of those who were there and by looking at events of the times though their eyes. The names of John Brown and William Clarke Quantrill may be familiar, but others are probably not well known to you. Nevertheless, these regular citizens played a key role in Kansas's Civil War history.

Debbie Bisel has done extensive research for this book, and she enables us to gain a better understanding of the nuances of these turbulent times through the words of the people caught up in them. You'll meet Isaac and Mary Cody. Traveling from Iowa to the Kansas Territory, they were looking forward to a new life. However, once Isaac's free state views became known to his neighbors, he was attacked by proslavery men and severely injured. Several quotes of those present at and after his stabbing give real context to the situation. Despite the constant fear for his life,

Isaac Cody and his family would not be deterred, either in their political views on slavery or in expanding their family and business.

We also get a glimpse of how Kansans thought about their "military obligations" through stories of initiative and courage. Shortly after statehood, and as rumors flew in Washington, D.C., about plots to capture President Lincoln at the start of the Civil War, one of Kansas's first senators took action. Senator James Henry Lane recruited the Frontier Guard, a group of Kansas volunteers in Washington, to protect the president. First headquartered in the Willard Hotel and then the East Room of the White House, these Kansans served for more than fifteen days until the Union army arrived to relieve them. The Frontier Guard was essentially the first Secret Service, an organization authorized by Lincoln after the war ended.

Here you'll learn how Kansans established the first Northern African American unit recruited to fight in the Civil War, the First Kansas Colored Infantry. These units were the first to see battle and the first to suffer casualties. Although these units didn't get the recognition of the Fifty-fourth Massachusetts (portrayed in the movie *Glory*), they fought with great distinction during the Civil War.

Kansas obtained statehood on January 29, 1861. The state motto "Ad astra per aspera" roughly means "To the stars through difficulty." What a descriptive and appropriate motto, reflecting the tumultuous road to becoming our thirty-fourth state. In these trying times, Debbie Bisel's book captures the story of Kansas and, at the same time, the story of our nation. This is a must read for those who think that they know their Civil War history.

Richard B. Myers
General, USAF, Retired

Preface

I remember the very night I became enamored of Kansas history. I was watching an Errol Flynn marathon on television: *The Adventures of Robin Hood, Don Juan, They Died With Their Boots On* and S*anta Fe Trail*—the last with Flynn as Jeb Stuart, my hometown (Ararat, Virginia) boy! And there he was in Kansas. With John Brown and Cyrus K. Holliday. I was mesmerized. It was late, and I was watching television by myself. Kansas sucked me in.

Years later, I found myself living in Topeka—temporarily, I thought. Because I am a native southerner, I acquainted myself with the town by walking through the graveyard. Situated on a hilltop on the east side of Topeka is the oldest incorporated cemetery in the state. The city skyline forms the background for the gravestones of those who built the city. I knew little of Topeka's history when I arrived, but I recognized the street names among the markers. Then I stumbled, literally, over the headstone of Cyrus Kurtz Holliday, the real man who had inspired such a colorful character in the movie. The scenes came back to me, and I wanted to know more. I looked around and wondered if Kansans were aware of what an incredible, historic and beautiful place rested at their doorstep. I felt as if I had found a hidden treasure, and I wanted to share it.

It was as if a door opened to a historic world; I earned a history degree at Washburn University and studied at the Buffalo Bill Historical Center in Cody, Wyoming, one summer. It, too, was a life-altering experience. William F. Cody's life was so representative of America's nineteenth century—he embodied Manifest Destiny, that belief that the United States could, and should, spread its boundaries and people from Atlantic to Pacific. His generous spirit knew no bounds. He took the American West to the world. I adore him.

I began to realize that all historic roads lead to Kansas, and I wanted to travel every one of them. From Bleeding Kansas to the Civil War and the Plains Indian wars, there is no more compelling time in our nation's history, and Kansas was the center of it, geographically and spiritually. Each road led to another: Jeb Stuart to Edwin Sumner to John Brown to Jim Lane to Abraham Lincoln—all one marvelous crisscrossing story.

No other state's history is so entwined with America's Civil War as that of Kansas. Born of the war, the cause of the war, Kansas exists as a monument to the "second birth of freedom" that freed millions of Americans and demonstrated that the bonds of Union were strong enough to survive the epic struggle.

While the Civil War officially lasted almost exactly four years, Kansas was at war for ten. To distill the people and events of those tumultuous times into a volume this size is impossible. It would be reduced to a glorified outline, if even that. Thus, I have elected to share some of the stories and people who are most meaningful to me, and I urge you to learn more. I do not claim to be objective, but I have tried to be fair and will hereby acknowledge to you where my prejudice is: I believe Kansas history is second to none.

That being said, the stories of Kansas and Missouri are likewise entwined and are usually told from very different perspectives. Each is valid, and I encourage you to look at the other side of the border. My apologies to all who are deserving and are not mentioned in this volume, and there are many.

With these few stories, I have attempted to place the Kansas experience in the broader context of America's story and to illustrate how interconnected the fate of Kansas was to that of the nation. How vital a piece of the Civil War puzzle is Kansas!

The history of the Kansas/Missouri border is so rich, so do not stop with this small book. Watch the documentaries *Bad Blood* and *Touched by Fire* on the Bleeding Kansas era. Read the numerous very well-written books on the subject. Become a reenactor. Join a historical society or a Civil War roundtable. Donate to a historic site. Become a docent.

History is like the nightly news: the tragedies get the headlines. As you read of the violence that marred the state's early years, I hope you realize that the real accomplishment is found in the lives of ordinary men and women who built homes and communities, schools and colleges, despite the chaos and fear; they never lost sight of the stars, no matter what their difficulties. I am privileged to know them, and I am honored to share them with you.

Acknowledgements

M any thanks to friends and fellow historians Bryce Benedict and Michelle Martin, who read through this manuscript and offered their expert insights. I am blessed to count among my friends many dedicated historians, reenactors, filmmakers and authors. They have all contributed to my understanding and enjoyment of history. Dale Vaughn generously allowed me to use his excellent map of early Kansas, first printed in his historic fiction, *Black Jack*. Thanks to Emory Cantey for allowing me to use his rare image of William Clarke Quantrill. I am indebted to Ryan Finn and Becky Lejeune of The History Press for their patience and expertise. Special thanks to my husband, who supports me in all things, and to my friends, who listen to me. I appreciate my daughter Karen for her pep talks and my daughter Noël, who helped me sort out piles of sources.

I am most indebted to those local historians who keep the flames of history burning in their little corners of the world. Whether it be Paul Bahnmeir, Tim Rues and the Lecompton Reenactors in Lecompton, Kansas, or Dan Hadley and his compatriots at Lone Jack, Missouri, these people give tirelessly of their time and talent so that people they may never know will have the opportunity to touch the past. The Black Jack Battlefield, nearly forgotten for decades, has become an important destination because of the group dedicated to its interpretation. There are so many other similar stories—the Ritchie House, Constitution Hall in Topeka, the Harris-Kearney House, Mount Mitchell Heritage Prairie, the Humboldt Museum, Little House on the Prairie, the Burnt District

Monument, the Bushwhacker Museum; there are so many great things happening in the historical community!

In anticipation of the 150th anniversary of the Civil War, Freedom's Frontier National Heritage Area was established in 2006. It is a thirty-one-thousand-square-mile section of eastern Kansas and western Missouri. It is the setting for the events described in this book. Please visit and support these historic sites. For more information, the organization's website is www.freedomsfrontier.org.

History has brought many dear friends into my life, and Philadelphia has become quite familiar to me. Our generous and knowledgeable friends, Dr. Anthony and Carol Waskie, live there and share not only their history but also their home. Likewise, Lieutenant Colonel (ret.) David and Teresa Chuber, Fort Leonard Wood, are constant sources of knowledge and inspiration. Lieutenant Colonel (ret.) Ed Kennedy is on call any time of the night or day, as is Colonel (ret.) Dennis K. Clark ("Deb's encyclopedia"), Douglass Wallace and William Wagnon.

And finally, my profound thanks to General Richard B. Myers (USAF, Ret.), Fifteenth Chairman of the Joint Chiefs of Staff, not only for writing the foreword to this book but also for his decades of service and devotion to our country. He makes Kansas proud to call him a native son.

The Kansas Image

The Kansas Statehouse is an impressive structure with a dome that rivals that of the Capitol in Washington, D.C. Its ornate wings house the chambers of government in a near palatial setting. In fact, the statehouse is decidedly un-Kansaslike in its personality. Kansans are not showoffs. They value results over appearances. They accomplish things quietly.

Each year, thousands of schoolchildren, from Wichita to White Cloud and from Gardner to Goodland, descend like hordes of locusts on the marble steps and leave fingerprints on the brass banisters. Their chatter echoes off the limestone. Frantic teachers herd them up to the second floor to view what will likely be the one sight pressed into their brains from the day's excursion: the towering image of John Brown, rifle in one outstretched hand, the Bible in his other. Underneath his feet are the bodies of two dead soldiers—one in blue, the other in gray. Around him, men pray and fight, waving different flags, as wagon trains roll past. Behind it all, a tornado and a prairie fire threaten the landscape. Yet John Brown towers above it all. There are gasps, moments of silence and then tons of questions. Who is he? Who are the men around him? Is the tornado going to get him? Will the prairie fire kill him? What does he have to do with Kansas? Why do they have guns? Is he a bad man? Is he crazy?

Historians ponder the same issues as schoolchildren. Native son John Steuart Curry was the natural choice when a group of newspaper editors spearheaded the effort to cover the walls of the statehouse with murals depicting the story of Kansas. Curry, along with Iowa's Grant Wood and Missouri's Thomas Hart Benton, made up America's greatest regionalist painters. The Curry homestead in Jefferson County was located on the Hickory Point Battlefield, the site of one of dozens of occasions that gave the territory the name "Bleeding Kansas." As a child, Curry would have been well aware of the area's legacy. He might have found a stray bullet or perhaps a rusted knife blade. He and the neighborhood children might have chosen sides and replayed those violent days. Whatever he did as a child, as an adult his work demonstrated the impact of having been born and reared on the war-worn soil of Kansas.

Curry went east, working at the Westport Art Colony in Connecticut. He achieved national recognition with his painting *Baptism in Kansas*. He was subsequently hired to transform the walls of several federal buildings in Washington, D.C. Curry was honored to have the opportunity to return to his native state and paint the Capitol's murals, but in the end, the experience would break his heart and, according to his widow, hasten his death.

Tragic Prelude, the painting with John Brown as its centerpiece, was Curry's greatest work—or at least he thought so. Born only forty years after John Brown launched his campaign of terror, Curry was shaped by the struggles with nature and the political strife that had formed Kansas.

Artist and actor Don Lambert formed a bond with Mrs. John Steuart Curry that resulted in many of Curry's works coming back to Kansas. *Don Lambert.*

"I want to paint this war with nature and I want to paint the things I feel as a native Kansan," Curry said when he was commissioned to paint the statehouse murals. Reflecting on the images, the artist added, "I sincerely believe that in…the panel of John Brown, I have accomplished the greatest paintings I have yet done, and that they will stand as historical monuments."

Many Kansans did not agree. They nitpicked the details of the paintings: the Hereford bull was not the right color; the tornado looked like the trunk of an elephant; and the pigs' tails did not curl enough. All of these criticisms were just dancing around the center of the issue, literally. The fact was that Kansans did not want the fanatic John Brown representing *them*.

In 1942, Curry refused to sign the murals and considered them unfinished. He left his native state, never to return, devastated that what had been a labor of love for him had been so maligned by his fellow Kansans. He died in Wisconsin in 1946.

Kansas actor and artist Don Lambert studied Curry's work and set out to correct the injustice done to one of the state's most talented sons. In 1990, Lambert went to Connecticut to visit the woman who had been Curry's wife for twelve years and his widow for half a century. He was not sure how she would receive him, but she welcomed Lambert into her home and her husband's legacy. She gave Lambert her blessing to portray Curry. Lambert informed her of the many fledgling efforts to restore her husband's reputation in Kansas. The two developed a lasting friendship.

Two years later, in celebration of the multimillion-dollar restoration of the building, the Kansas legislature hosted Lambert as Curry. He was wearing white, paint-spattered coveralls and looked strikingly like the famous artist. The chambers were quiet as the legislature reflected on his performance and the actions of their predecessors fifty years earlier. They gave Lambert a standing ovation and passed a resolution of apology to John Steuart Curry.

Lambert arranged for a $100,000 legislative appropriation to buy seventeen Curry sketches done in preparation for the mural. Mrs. Curry was so impressed by the efforts that she cut the price in half and added three other drawings to the deal. She continued to donate items, including substantial gifts to the Beach Museum of Art at K-State, with the certainty that her husband was finally going to be recognized and appreciated in his homeland.

Curry had correctly foreseen the impact of his work when he called the murals "historical monuments." It is a pity that he could not enjoy the recognition and reverence that his work would one day command.

Tragic Prelude is the work of native son John Steuart Curry, who was commissioned to cover the walls of the Kansas Statehouse with images from Kansas history. He believed that it was his greatest work, although it was unappreciated at the time. *Kansas State Historical Society.*

Author Bryce Benedict recalled how the image had towered over him as a child. "I had no idea who he [John Brown] was or why he was up there," he said, "but I would never forget his face and those outstretched arms." He was inspired to find out who the larger-than-life character was. As he became immersed in history, Benedict came to understand Brown's role, both in Kansas and in the nation. "I think that mural aptly portrays how Kansas was born in blood," Benedict added. "The mural defines Bleeding Kansas."

William C. Davis, prolific author on the Civil War, commented that "in the 1850s, [John Brown] and Kansas became synonymous. They remain so since." He added, "Whether one regards him as a freedom fighter or the first of the modern terrorists, John Brown is a mountain in the path of history.

One simply cannot go around him. Anyone on that path must confront the man and what he did on those prairies that made them together a milestone on another road to turmoil, war, and freedom."

For Kansans, John Brown is inescapable. In the 1970s, when the homegrown rock band Kansas launched their musical career, it was Curry's *Tragic Prelude* that they chose for their debut album cover. Founding band member Kerry Livgren commented, "Since we were kids we all saw that mural in the statehouse. It was simply a link identifying us with our homeland." Livgren added that after all this time, he hasn't changed his mind. "I would use it again."

Like Livgren, most Kansans have come to value the work of John Steuart Curry and realize that he did capture what it means to be a Kansan. It would appear then, from the images, that being a Kansan entails great struggle. As another great Kansan, Greg Case,[1] said, "Opportunity is born out of turmoil."

That turmoil began with the Kansas-Nebraska Act.

Chapter 1

A Peaceful Valley

Isaac Cody was not idly waiting for the passage of the Kansas-Nebraska Act. He had already obtained permission to put up a "cheep [*sic*] cabin" in the Kansas Territory and had signed a government contract to supply hay to Fort Leavenworth. He was ferrying his family across the Missouri River to their temporary home when he received the dispatch that President Pierce had signed the law almost two weeks earlier, on May 30, 1854. The next day, he unpacked his surveying tools and began outlining land claims.

Isaac and his wife, Mary, had begun planning this trip in the previous fall. A young son had died after a fall from a horse, and Mary was disconsolate. This move was just the sort of distraction that the family needed. Isaac's correspondence with Iowa congressmen informed him that the bill creating the new territory would likely be voted on during the winter session. Isaac was by no means a nomad, but he had made more than one move seeking a better life and had enjoyed some financial success. When the Codys loaded their six surviving children into a wagon and left Iowa, they did not camp along the roadside at night, as did most other pioneers, but were instead able to afford the "best hotels" along the way.

Crossing the state line into Missouri, the children encountered black people for the first time, most of them slaves or servants. They were a great curiosity to the children, and they asked if these were Indians.

Isaac's brother, Elijah Cody, was a successful businessman in Weston, Missouri. He encouraged his brother to come west and told him that it was a beautiful country. The Kansas countryside in spring did not disappoint the

Codys. Riding out to "Government Hill" at Fort Leavenworth, the family saw the Salt Creek Valley for the first time: "[I]t was filled with Trains and cattle and mules running around. There must have been Hundreds of White covered wagons waiting there to make up their Train to start West," wrote

The Kansas/Missouri border in 1856. *Dale Vaughn.*

Julia Cody Goodman. "Father and Mother both made the remark that if they could get their house in that beautiful valley, there would be their Home."[2]

The Codys soon learned that a Kansas spring is not to be trusted. The climate can turn at any moment, but the political climate may have been far more dangerous.

Most of the early settlers in that area of the Kansas Territory supported the extension of slavery. One could almost throw a rock from Missouri to the territory when the river was down, and thus many Missourians had their eyes on that "beautiful valley" for a long time, just waiting for the federal government's blessing to lay stake to it. Young Willie Cody (later in life the world-famous "Buffalo Bill") recalled that many of those proslavers came over with whiskey and, when the bottles were empty, drove them into the ground to mark their claim.[3]

Ironically, on the same day the Codys arrived, settlers were gathering at the Kickapoo Indian trading post to organize into the Salt Creek Squatters Association. It was a common practice to establish some order in the land claim business. A register of claims and a board to handle disputes were appointed, in addition to a "vigilance" committee (which included Isaac) to enforce decisions. Another item of business was the treatment of abolitionists. The vigilantes would make sure that abolitionists were not welcome in this neighborhood.[4] This is one example of the many groups organized in the image of a governmental entity with no governmental authority whatsoever. The only true power they possessed was that of the gun.

Isaac Cody was included in this group because his neighbors assumed that his politics would be the same as his brother's. Elijah Cody was not only a prominent businessman in Weston, but he was also a prominent slaveholder. They soon found differently, though.

"Father was a plain spoken man," Julia Cody Goodman recalled, "and these Missourians soon found out how Father stood on that as they would go back and tell about Elijah Cody's Brother being for Kansas to be a Free state, and they would come back and howl the slander about Father. But he would [continue to] talk."[5]

Isaac went about his business and hired several men to fill his hay contracts with the fort. In all his dealings, he made no attempt to disguise his political views. In the middle of September, Isaac was traveling between his home and Fort Leavenworth. A crowd of mostly proslavery advocates started to heckle Isaac and demanded a speech.

"He tried to beg off," said Julia, "offering every excuse." They grabbed him, put him atop a freight box and then began shouting questions at him:

> *One of the men called out, You are the man that wants Kansas Territory to be a Free state, don't you? He went on talking on various questions and some one called out again, Say, Cody, you want to make Kansas a free state. He sayed yes. With that a man jumped on the Box and called him a Damed Abolicetionist and grabed at him.*[6]

Young Willie was likely not present, but his later memoirs carried a description of the incident, probably a combination of the accounts he was told. He wrote that the crowd was hissing and shouting:

> *"You black abolitionist, shut up!" "Get down from that box!" "Kill him!" "Shoot him!" and so on. Father, however, maintained his position on the*

William F. "Buffalo Bill" Cody, circa 1858, at about twelve years old. Cody's father, Isaac, was one of the first martyrs to the cause of abolitionism. *Kansas State Historical Society.*

dry-goods box, notwithstanding the excitement and the numerous invitations to step down, until a hot-headed pro-slavery man, who was in the employ of my Uncle Elijah, crowded up and said: "Get off that box, you black abolitionist, or I'll pull you off."

Father paid but little attention to him, and attempted to resume his speech, intending doubtless to explain his position and endeavor to somewhat pacify the angry crowd. But the fellow jumped up on the box, and pulling out a huge bowie knife, stabbed father twice, who reeled and fell to the ground. The man sprang after him, and would have ended his life then and there, had not some of the better men in the crowd interfered in time to prevent him from carrying out his murderous intention.[7]

Julia said that as her father fell, a neighbor, Dr. Hathaway, "got to him and they took him in to the store and he done what he could for him. They did not try to do anything with this man, Mr. Dunn. They broke up the meeting."[8]

Mrs. Cody was summoned, and it was decided that Isaac should not go home but rather should go to Elijah's home to recuperate. It was considered safer there, an ironic conclusion since the Charles Dunn (who had done the stabbing) was employed by Elijah Cody. Bill's memoirs reflected, "My uncle of course at once discharged the ruffian from his employ."[9]

Young Willie did not record his reaction to his father's stabbing, but his sister, Julia, did. Julia recalled that Willie (a child of only eight at the time) "would cry and then he would say, Oh, I wish I was a man; I would just love to kill all of those Bad men that want to kill my Father, and I will when I get big."[10]

Missouri newspapers took a somewhat different view of Dunn's actions. From the *Democratic Platform* in Liberty:

A Mr. Cody, a noisy abolitionist, living near Salt Creek in Kansas Territory, was severely stabbed, while in a dispute about a claim with Mr. Dunn, on Monday week last. Cody is severely hurt, but not enough it is feared to cause his death. The settlers on Salt Creek regret that his wound is not more dangerous and all sustain Mr. Dunn in the course he took. Abolitionists will yet find "Jordan a hard road to travel."[11]

According to all accounts recorded by the family, the next few months were full of "misfortunes and difficulties." Proslavery gangs showed up at the Cody home periodically to finish the job that Dunn had started, but Isaac would not be deterred from his work. Often forced to hide or travel with escorts, he helped establish Grasshopper Falls as a free state community. His visits to his family were all too brief and often interrupted. He sometimes left his horse with a neighbor and walked home to avoid detection, and he was often ill, never fully healing from the stab wounds. Julia Cody Goodman recalled one of those rare times at home when her father lay in bed, sick:

> The next day he was not able to get up and was in bed up stairs and as mother and sister Martha were sitting there a man rode up to the Door and threw the reighns [reins] off of his Horses neck and he walked in and asked mother to fix him some Dinner. So Sister Martha went to fixing it for him. He asked mother where that Damd Abolitionist Husband was and that he had the Knife, and he took out of the scabrt [scabbard] and sharpened on his whet stone and sayed that was to take his heart's blood wherever he could find him.
>
> Mother spoke up; she sayed, Julia, you and Willie take the children up stairs. We went up, took the 3 sisters up stairs. Father had heard all that had been sayed. He sayed, Now you will have to protect me as I am too sick. Willie, you get your gun—it always stood behind the closet door—and Julia you get that ax, and Father sayed, Now if that man starts to come up stairs, Willie, you shoot, and Julia, if Willie misses him, you hit him with the ax, for he might deside to search the House.
>
> But mother talked to him while he was Eating and after he got through he looked around and sayed, I see something I can make use of. That was Father's Leather sadle bags. He took them down and sayed, When ever that Damd Abolitionist comes in we will be on the Look out for him and we will fix him as we are gone to kill ever one of these Abolitionists until we clear this Territory of them; and then he left...We had to be on the watch all the time when ever he was home.[12]

In such a climate, it is difficult to imagine how any kind of ordinary life existed or how one could maintain the commitment to political ideals. The Codys did both. They continued to plant crops and raise livestock, despite theft and destruction. And the family continued to grow.

In May 1855, Mary Cody gave birth to a boy, named Charles Whitney in honor of one of the other founders of Grasshopper Falls. Word spread to the two nearby Indian tribes. The Kickapoo chief brought gifts of beads, moccasins and other Indian playthings. Mrs. Cody responded by giving him some sugar. Several days later, according to Julia, the Delaware chief arrived, also bearing gifts, and he also received a reciprocal gift of sugar. The Delaware chief also made it plain that the Kickapoo chief had usurped his position by visiting the Codys, as it was the Delaware who had dominion. It was one memory of territorial Kansas that the Codys could look back on and smile.

Chapter 2

That "Damned Yankee Town"

J oseph Savage was one of about sixty brave souls who left Boston for the Kansas Territory in August 1854. A smaller group had left in July. His heart was heavy at having to leave his family behind, but his spirits were buoyed by the hearty cheers of the townspeople as the train left the depot. The band played "Oh! Susanna" and "Auld Lang Syne," which was sung with new verses. A card with a printed poem was passed to the enthusiastic well-wishers, and this would become the anthem of the free state settlers. Penned by John Greenleaf Whittier, the words recalled the spirit of America's founding:

> *We cross the prairie as of old,*
> *The pilgrims cross the sea,*
> *To make the West, as they the East,*
> *The homestead of the free!*
> *We go to rear a wall of men*
> *On Freedom's southern line,*
> *And plant beside the cotton tree*
> *The rugged northern pine!*

"[T]he song was sung by many with tears in their eyes," recalled Savage.

Savage studied his travel mates. "A few were enthusiastic young men, willing, and perhaps anxious, to become martyrs to their principles—who would go out of their way to let pro-slavery men know their sentiments," he speculated. "But most were modest, quiet men—men of brains and backbone."

Traveling hundreds of miles by rail, the group boarded a steamer at Buffalo, New York, and crossed Lake Erie to Detroit. The ride proved a ripe opportunity for speeches and resolutions regarding their future in Kansas. It was considered a particularly good omen when a little bird flew onto the boat. It was likened to the journey of Columbus, alerted that land was near by the presence of a bird. The travelers finally reached the Mississippi River, where they joyfully bathed and boarded a steamer headed for St. Louis and then another steamer that would take them to Kansas City and beyond.

"We arrived at Kansas City just seven days from Boston, and were provided with cotton tents of the Aid Society," Savage recorded, "and camped by a nice spring of water just north of the city, over the line in Kansas Territory."

The travelers, now so near their destination, purchased provisions and wagons and set out to see this magnificent country. Having read accounts in the newspapers that all Yankees who attempted to enter Kansas through Westport would be shot, there was some trepidation and the men armed themselves. With guns shouldered, the ferocious northerners bought cider and gingerbread and headed to Kansas.

The land was timbered for several miles, and then the group saw the Kansas prairie laid out before them like a carpet. Savage swung his hat over his head and shouted, "Glory! Glory!" at the sight. The men linked arms and strode into the grass, singing with "unbounded satisfaction":

> *We cross the prairies as of old*
> *Our fathers crossed the sea...*

Charles Robinson and S.C. Pomeroy, agents of the society, went ahead and chose the site for the new town. Robinson was no stranger to this land, having traveled this very road years before on his way to California. He selected his old campsite to locate the new town.

On September 16, 1854, Savage and his fellow travelers arrived on Mount Oread and found what remained of the first immigrant party living in tents and drinking brackish water from a nearby ravine. Still, they were optimistic. On their second night in Kansas, a terrific thunderstorm occurred.

"Our tents had been staked in haste, carelessly," wrote Savage, "so that they reeled to and fro in the wind like a ship in mid-ocean. Each one of the five occupying our tent seized its flapping folds, and held with might and main the cord to their places."

Charles Robinson, a physician who tired of sick people, was committed not only to making Kansas a free state but also to the founding of a university. He selected the spot, Mount Oread, long before the University of Kansas became a reality. *Kansas State Historical Society.*

The next morning, one of their number packed up and headed back east. Those remaining met at Mount Oread to establish the association that would plot out and govern the city. Again the weather ruled. "The day was rather windy," wrote Savage, "and, it being so difficult to hear each other, we adjourned over the point of the bluff to the south."

Great consideration was given to the name of this city when Caleb Pratt proposed naming it in honor of Amos Lawrence, one of the wealthy industrialists who had helped found the Emigrant Aid Society. Pratt pragmatically pointed out that it would be gratifying to Lawrence and would encourage him to make other bequests for schools and libraries. Robinson heartily agreed, and it was unanimously decided by the seventy-nine men present that Lawrence would be the name.

In time, the honor bestowed on him would cost Amos Lawrence thousands of dollars.[13]

THE KANSAS NEBRASKA ACT

It was a foregone conclusion that Kansas would be a slave state. That was the natural order of things: Pennsylvanians settled Ohio, and Ohioans settled Indiana; North Carolinians settled Tennessee, and Tennesseans settled Arkansas; Virginians settled Kentucky, and Kentuckians settled Missouri; and Missiourians would settle Kansas. Since the landing of Europeans, the original thirteen colonies had claim on the lands to the west of them. As the march westward went farther and farther, an argument arose about extending slavery into that vast desert. As the land and climate became more and more different in the Great Plains, many people thought slavery impractical in the western reaches of America; others could not imagine working the land on any grand scale without slave labor. The first real test of the traditional patterns of settlement came when Missouri entered the Union.

In 1820, Congress danced around the issue of expanded slavery by passing the Missouri Compromise. Endeavoring to keep a balance of slave and free states, Congress brilliantly decided to prohibit slavery throughout the former Louisiana Purchase north of the 36°30' parallel *except* for the proposed state of Missouri.

As is often the case, the politicians again took the cowardly way out with the Kansas-Nebraska Act. Rather than taking a firm stand in Washington, the issue would be decided by popular sovereignty. What could be more appropriate than allowing the citizens themselves to decide?

As one settler said, "The Kansas law providing for a state government is, upon its face, a fair law."[14] On its face, perhaps, but it was not fair in its practical application. Actually, its practical application in a "fair" manner proved impossible.

Missouri anticipated the bill's passage. Missourians merely had to walk over the border or ferry across the Missouri River and stake a claim, and many did so even before the territory was technically open. Anyone with

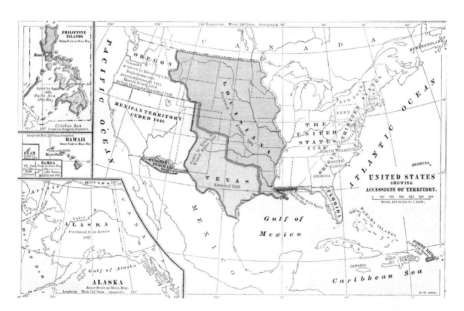

The Louisiana Purchase made by President Thomas Jefferson in 1803 virtually doubled the size of the United States. Missouri and Kansas were both carved from that territory. *Author's collection.*

any motivation at all could stake a claim and vote in the elections, and if the weather or politics did not suit them, they could cut their losses and head home. If it worked out well, they could stay in Kansas and prosper. Kansas would become an extension of Missouri and, therefore, a slave state. (The abolitionists could have Nebraska.) Thus the passage of the Kansas-Nebraska Act was interpreted as supporting the extension of slavery.

Senator William Seward of New York voiced the outrage and determination of northerners. "Come on then, gentlemen of the Slave States," stormed Seward. "Since there is no escaping your challenge, I accept it in behalf of the cause of freedom. We will engage in competition for the virgin soil of Kansas, and God give the victory to the side which is stronger in numbers as it is in the right."[15]

If numbers would decide the day, the abolitionists of New England were determined to alter history. They would not be foiled by the maneuvers of greedy politicians. If voters would decide the fate of Kansas, then New England would send voters—lots of voters.

The Kansas-Nebraska Act, carving those territories from the Louisiana Purchase, was signed by President Franklin Pierce on May 30, 1854. Though the chief executive was from New Hampshire, he was inclined to favor southern interests on many issues. His signing what was considered to be a proslavery bill was the last straw for many of his constituents in the North.

The bill was primarily authored by the senator from Illinois, Stephen A. Douglas, himself a native of Vermont, who is best remembered for making Abraham Lincoln a household name through the Lincoln-Douglas debates. Rather than being applauded for his solution, he became vilified in the North.

"Senator Douglas, as he returned to his home in Illinois, saw men and boys along the way burning his picture as a protest against his leadership in the matter," wrote one historian. "He declared he was lighted all the way home from Washington by the glare of his own burning effigies."[16]

"Whether one agreed with it or not," noted Nicole Etcheson, "Kansas-Nebraska invested the territory's residents with the right to make a momentous political decision."[17]

"If the purpose of the enactment was to quiet the agitation of the slavery question, it signally failed," wrote historian Noble L. Prentiss. "The direct result of the introduction of the Kansas-Nebraska Act was to bring on a discussion more violent and widespread than had ever been before known in the country. As far as the conflict affected the Nation at large, the details belong to the general political history of the United States. The centre and most perilous spot in the field was soon transferred to Kansas Territory."[18]

Chapter 3

Propaganda and Privation

On December 5, 1854, Thomas Hart Benton, the U.S. senator from Missouri, addressed an audience in Maryland, extolling the virtues of the Kansas Territory, which possessed a "soil rich like Egypt!" He had voted against the Kansas-Nebraska Act, but now that it was law, he aimed to make the most of it and acknowledged the "great political rights" the law afforded citizens who settled there. He noted that foreign immigrants would take advantage of these policies and expected the country to fill up quickly, a good thing for the progress of the United States. But the crowning reason to settle Kansas was, according to Benton, the "Pacific Railroad!"

"Kanzas has the charter from nature for that road, and will use it," Benton told the Marylanders. "She has the smooth way on which to place it—the straight way on which to run it—the material with which to build it—the soil and people to support it—and the salubrious climate to give it exemption from diseases."[19]

"The whole route for the road between the States of Missouri and California is good—not only good, but supremely excellent," continued Benton, "and it is helped out at each end by water lines of transportation, now actually existing, and by railways, projected, or in progress. At the Missouri end there is a railway in construction to the line of the State and steamboat navigation to the mouth of the Kanzas, and up that river some hundred miles."[20]

Benton continued to plot out the course and impact of this grand plan:

The road will be made, and soon, and by individual enterprize. The age is progressive and utilitarian. It abounds with talent, seeking employment, and with capital, seeking investment. The temptation is irresistible. To reach the golden California—to put the populations of the Atlantic, the Pacific, and the Mississippi Valley, into direct communion—to connect Europe and Asia through our America—and to own a road of our own to the East Indies: such is the grandeur of the enterprize! And the time has arrived to begin it…The world is in motion, following the track of the sun to its dip in the western ocean. Westward the torrents of emigration direct their course; and soon the country between Missouri and California is to show the most rapid expansion of the human race that the ages of man have ever beheld.[21]

The idea of a transcontinental railroad carried the potential for prosperity that was absolutely intoxicating. Every campaign promise, every banking venture, every speculator's dream in the midst of the nineteenth century was built on the iron rail. This brought men and women from every walk of life to the Kansas Territory. Had there not been economic opportunity, there would have been no conflict over slavery. No one would have been interested in moving to Kansas if they had not believed they could prosper financially.

Flush with money from a railroad investment in Pennsylvania, Cyrus K. Holliday set his sights on the Kansas Territory. Youthful, idealistic and educated, Holliday was just the sort of man promoters hoped to attract, and the settlement of the American West was just the opportunity ambitious entrepreneurs were looking for. The timeline was all worked out in Holliday's head: settle Kansas, bring Kansas into the Union as a free state and build a railroad. It was simple.

Holliday briefly made his home with the free staters of Lawrence. Perhaps he thought that the choicest lands had already been claimed in that community or maybe his motivation was political, but whatever his reasoning, he chose to leave Lawrence in favor of founding another town. He did believe that another settlement would strengthen the free state party's hold on the territory. Thus, he and eight other men met on "the soil rich as Egypt," about thirty miles upriver from Lawrence, and established one of those western outposts that Senator Benton, at that very moment, was urging Marylanders to settle.

It was an inglorious beginning. A shabby cabin, made from the trunks of "small, crooked" trees with a roof of brush and prairie grass, had been constructed on the south side of the Kansas River. A short distance up the stream, Papan's Ferry carried travelers bound westward on the Oregon Trail. The men who found themselves assembled in the cabin were virtual strangers to one another, according to the recollection of Fry Giles. In fact, Cyrus Holliday was singled out to speak not because of his comrades' knowledge of his abilities, but because he wore a white hat.

It is probably not a stretch to assume that he was also very eager. There was no furniture, only a few provisions. Thus, atop a sack of flour, the grand plan for Topeka was announced. Rather, the grand plan for a *general* town was announced. They were unconcerned initially in naming their creation. However, these founding fathers began to

Ambitious and optimistic, Cyrus K. Holliday was a founder of Topeka in addition to the Atchison, Topeka and Santa Fe Railroad. His unfailing commitment to expanding Topeka was a large factor in the city's becoming the state capital. *Great Overland Station.*

fear that the proslavery faction would name the town something inappropriate that would stick in the minds of the public and be very difficult to erase from the memory. Apparently, this had happened in other locales, so they were moved to act. One of the men suggested the perfect name, one that was not found in any post office of the United States nor in any dictionary of the English language. He, in fact, had just heard it for the first time from the mouth of another settler who might have heard it from an Indian. The word "Topeka" was unique and easy to pronounce. It was adopted. The discussions then turned to the street names. Tree names were tossed aside for those of presidents, except for the unpopular President Franklin Pierce, who was tossed aside in favor of General John C. Frémont.

"[T]he name of Pierce would not be tolerated for a moment," wrote Fry Giles, "on account of the policy of his administration toward Kansas."[22]

Topeka's founders were full of energy and optimism and immediately went to work surveying the town with a fifty-cent compass and scraps of rope that had been tied around their provisions. (A more accurate government survey was completed later.)

Charles Robinson of Massachusetts, an agent of the New England Emigrant Aid Society, was instrumental in founding Topeka, but he returned to Lawrence soon after Topeka was established. Holliday then became an acting agent of the society. In later years, Fry Giles sought to dispel the notion that Topeka had been one of the communities founded by this organization. Perhaps he wanted to emphasize the individual efforts and sacrifices of Topeka's founders. The privations they endured were remarkable. Just days after the town association was established, Holliday wrote to his wife, who had remained in Pennsylvania until he could send for her:

> [I]*f you know the inconveniences under which I write you would almost excuse me from writing at all—I am now better situated for writing than I have been in, perhaps, any other occasion; and I am now sitting upon a trunk with a box…before me as my desk—at this moment the Minister who has just preached for us—and who is lying upon my bed, which consists of a handful of hay and a Buffalo Robe, by accident, has almost kicked my desk over—and while writing the last line I have removed twice—once to get out of our cooks way—and once to get nearer the door for light—our cabin having no windows in it.*[23]

From Holliday's first moment in the territory, there was no doubt that Kansas would be his permanent home. Only weeks after arriving, he identified himself not only geographically but also emotionally with his newfound land (emphasis added). *"You Pennsylvania people,"* Holliday wrote to his wife, "would be greatly surprised could you have a view of us as we find ourselves situated in this new Territory—In our new city—I would not exchange Kansas…for Penna with all its elegance & refinement."[24] Mrs. Holliday may have been amused or chagrined by her husband's including her with a suddenly "foreign" group, Pennsylvanians, since he had been one only a short time before.

As amusing as the statement is on the surface, however, it does reflect Holliday's feeling of having been transformed by the Kansas experience. This may have been the most important relationship of his life. It is to Mary's credit that she agreed to join her husband—if he had been forced to choose between her or Kansas, it would have been a close competition.

Part of the "Kansas experience" was common to pioneers of every era and locale. The absence of creature comforts, for example, was a common complaint from the founding of America. Fears of the elements, the natives and the unknown were universal. What was unique to those arriving in the Kansas Territory was the political climate in which the pioneering occurred. It was like an umbrella over every event, a rug that could be pulled out from under any accomplishment. It was a motivator for people to homestead in Kansas; it was reason many did not come.

As historian Craig Miner noted, "The process of the transformation of Kansas from wilderness to 'historic ground' was as much mental and spiritual as physical and political."[25] Such was certainly the case with Holliday. A young man of means and ability, he could have settled elsewhere, gone back to Pennsylvania or done any number of things without involving himself in the trials and tribulations of Kansas. It was love at first sight.

"God might have made a better country than Kansas," wrote Holliday, "but so far as my knowledge extends he certainly never did—I am bound to make it my home."[26]

The first test of Holliday's fidelity came but days after his intentions were declared. Holliday and his comrades had bedded down in their crude cabin. They slept in their clothes on piles of hay with buffalo robes for cover. There was some conversation about the flames from the chimney coming dangerously close to the roof, but all were tired and no one deemed it an emergency. They had not slept long when a flash of light woke them. The grass and thatch of the roof was on fire, with sparks falling to the hay beneath them. They scrambled to drag their meager provisions, including a keg of gunpowder, to safety. In the confusion, the molasses was spilled into the cornmeal and onto their clothes. The cabin was gone in minutes, and the night was young. There was a small tent that provided shelter to some while the others escaped the winter winds in a thicket of brush.[27]

"I am enduring almost every thing that it is possible for a man to endure; yet notwithstanding this I enjoy it all well," wrote the ever-optimistic Holliday. "This is certainly a most delightful country—I doubt whether even sunny and far famed Italy can favorably compare with this."[28]

Some folks who have endured severe Kansas winters might think that Holliday was delusional. Records indicate, however, that the winter of 1854–55 was unusually mild, with temperatures at about seventy on Christmas Day. Most of the accounts of the territory were made by travelers who

Constitution Hall was one of the first buildings constructed in Topeka and was the meeting place for the free state legislature that was dismissed by Colonel Edwin Sumner on July 4, 1856. After Kansas achieved statehood, it served as the seat of government while the state capitol was under construction. The building stands yet today as one of the key sites in the interpretation of the struggles over the destiny of Kansas. *Kansas State Historical Society.*

avoided the trails during the winter, so many settlers were taken by surprise with the 1855–56 season. Cyrus K. Holliday and his associates would need all this optimism and more in the trials to come, starting with the weather.

John and Mary Jane Ritchie came from Indiana in the spring of 1855, bringing their son, Hale, and baby, Mary. Ritchie purchased a share of the town from Enoch Chase and quickly went to work to establish a homestead if not a home. That fall found the Ritchies living in little more than a lean-to on the banks of the Shunganunga Creek. Taking scraps of lumber from Holliday, they dug into the hillside and erected a crude cabin. Damp, drafty and cold, their living conditions may have contributed to the death of their little girl in October. Mary Jane would recall that water froze in the glasses on the table and bread had to be thawed over the fire before it could be sliced.[29]

Indeed, Reverend Samuel Young Lum wrote from Lawrence in December 1855 that "the thermometer has been within a week as low as 24° below zero; and it is about impossible to keep warm enough to write."[30]

People longed for spring, but had they known the events to come, they might have preferred to remain huddled by their fires. The warm temperatures would bring relief from the cold, but it would usher in a period of violence so profound that even the *Times* of London, England, would declare on its front page, "War in Kansas!"

Chapter 4

Old Osawatomie

John Brown's time in the Kansas Territory was short, just three years out of his fifty-nine on this earth. But in those tumultuous years, Brown left an indelible imprint on Kansas, and in turn, Kansas transformed John Brown into a legend. While the motives of others may have been vague or varied, John Brown's was not: he came to end slavery at any cost.

Veterans of the American Revolution would have been common when Brown was a boy. Born in Connecticut in 1800, Brown was raised in Hudson, Ohio, what was then the "Western Reserve," a piece of the nation's first "northwest." This was the edge of the frontier. During the War of 1812, Brown was helping to drive cattle to feed the army at Detroit. It was this trip that opened his eyes and imagination to slavery. He saw a slave boy, near his own age, being brutally whipped. He would never forget the incident. While opposed to slavery thereafter, it was the Kansas Territory that offered him the opportunity to direct all his energies to the abolition of slavery. While some only opposed the extension of slavery into Kansas, Brown saw this as the opportunity to make war on slavery itself, to strike such a blow that it would not be allowed to remain in *any* part of the nation.

Brown had bred his own army. The father of twenty children from two wives, Brown counted his family among his most devout followers. They, like their father, would be willing martyrs in the cause.

Brown arrived in Kansas in early October 1855. No one took notice except his family. His sons—John Jr., Jason, Owen, Frederick and Salmon—had been in the territory since February and had urged their

John Brown came to the Kansas Territory with his family determined not just to keep slavery from spreading but to abolish it altogether. He was active in the Underground Railroad but was controversial for his role in leading the Pottawatomie Massacre, in which five settlers were murdered. He was hanged for treason in Virginia in 1859. He had hoped to arm slaves in that area and start a rebellion. *Kansas State Historical Society.*

father to join them. They reported on the progress of the proslavery settlers and bemoaned their living conditions. They needed guns, they told their father, more than they needed bread, though neither was to be had in abundance. Brown was distressed to find his sons sick and living in makeshift tents.

"We found our folks in a most uncomfortable situation," Brown wrote to his wife, "with no Houses to shelter one of them; no Hay or Corn fodder of any account secured shivering over their little fires all exposed to the dreadfully cutting Winds Morning and Evening, & stormy days."[31]

Brown's introduction to the Great Plains was a rude one. "We were all out a good part of the night last," he wrote to his wife, "helping to keep the Prairie fires from destroying every thing so that I am almost blind today; or I would write you more." Nor did he waste any time taking up his cause. His letter continued, "Last Tuesday was an Election day with Free State men in Kansas, & hearing that there [was] a prospect of difficulty we all turned out most thoroughly armed."[32] The troublesome Missourians did not show up, and Brown took this as an encouraging sign that Missouri was "fast becoming discouraged about making Kansas a Slave State."[33]

The father was doing everything in his power to improve the living conditions for his family before winter struck in full force, but he did not focus much of his attention on matters of homesteading, planting or building. No, Brown had other abilities to offer Kansas, and they would soon come to light.

FUGITIVES

John Brown said of him, "I believe Montgomery to be a good man, but he has a mind of a peculiar mould."[34]

It is difficult to imagine what kind of man Brown would characterize as "peculiar," but James Montgomery fit the bill. An antislavery Missourian, Montgomery matched Brown in religious fervor, even if they did not interpret the scriptures in the quite the same way. Montgomery had been a schoolteacher, and like Brown, he came from the Western Reserve area of Ohio. He had also lived in Kentucky and Missouri, two slaveholding states, and had contact with slaveholders. He was reportedly not a fanatic in his views before moving to Kansas. He was sometimes given to preach a sermon or two.

Montgomery had not been particularly successful financially. When the Kansas Territory opened, he had two children (whose mother had died) and a new wife and not much else to take to a new homestead.

Whether by design or sheer bad luck, Montgomery's homestead was surrounded by proslavery settlers who did not make him welcome. His home was burned, but rather than being frightened away, the stubborn Montgomery became more entrenched and determined. As historian Brian Dirck pointed out, perhaps Montgomery's antislavery views hardened into real conviction—or maybe he just could not afford to move again. He built a new cabin, dubbed "Fort Montgomery," with vertical logs so tightly aligned that a bullet could not pass through, and he equipped it with an escape tunnel. He recruited other like-minded settlers to form another of

James Montgomery was an ardent abolitionist and friend of John Brown. He and his followers made southeastern Kansas an inhospitable environment for slave catchers trying to enforce the Fugitive Slave Act. *Kansas State Historical Society.*

the paramilitary groups that had become so popular along the Kansas-Missouri border.[35]

While some of these groups might have had legitimate reasons for existing (real lawmen or soldiers were rarely close by when needed), they often turned into bands as lawless and dangerous as any they were designed to counter. Such is the case with Montgomery, and he soon gained notoriety, even with other free staters. He led raids into Missouri, ostensibly against proslavery farms and towns. Men directly under Montgomery's command burned barns and crops and sometimes "stole" slaves as well. Montgomery was especially harsh on the slave hunters who came into the Kansas Territory to enforce the Fugitive Slave Act. Federal law still recognized slaves as property, and those who helped free slaves were criminals just as were horse thieves. Slave hunters received bounties for returning slaves to their owners. This could be especially lucrative where slaveholding and free states bordered one another, as with Kansas and Missouri, although slave catchers sometimes went as far north as Canada to retrieve property. Thus, even slaves who had escaped to "freedom" were often forced to look over their shoulders. Montgomery's intolerance of these men in the territory turned into terrifying defiance. In another example of a quasi-government group, Montgomery "arraigned" slave catchers before a jury of Jayhawkers. When convicted, most were allowed to leave, although at least one was executed.[36]

One of the interesting characteristics of the Kansas Territory was that just as a person's politics or religion would have been widely known, it would have also been known who were slave catchers and who were operators of the Underground Railroad (that series of safe houses used by escaping slaves). For example, proslavery posses often stopped at the home of John and Mary Jane Ritchie in Topeka, knowing that they often harbored runaway slaves. There were no secrets concerning people's actions; the only secret would have been knowing precisely when to catch someone. There were so many groups patrolling the countryside, with authority real or assumed, pity the poor pioneer just trying to live peaceably and remain neutral.

Chapter 5

Air Castles

The occupation of Kansas had begun. "The border counties of Missouri rang with the note of preparation," wrote one historian. "'Defensive Associations,' 'Squatters' Associations,' 'Blue Lodges' and various secret and open societies were formed on the border for the purpose of occupying Kansas, and the repelling of invaders of the abolition variety."[37] Other southern states followed suit, "some being sent from as far away as South Carolina, Alabama, Georgia and Florida."[38]

New York, Connecticut and Pennsylvania—even the nation's capital— urged settlement of the new territory. The New England Emigrant Aid Society was chartered on April 24, 1854, before the Kansas-Nebraska Act was signed into law. After the bill had passed the House of Representatives, its passage by the Senate and approval by the president seemed certain. New Englanders therefore wasted no time in using the features of the law itself to undermine its intent.

Whatever their starting place, pioneers north and south often found themselves together on the steamers headed up the Missouri River from St. Louis. The "Gateway to the West" was truly a transportation hub, with steamboats coming up and down the Mississippi and railroads coming from points north, south and east. One hundred years ago, a single word would have disclosed a passenger's background and, likely, their politics, as accents were much more pronounced. Clothing would have had a much more regional flair as well. Foreign immigrants, many from Ireland and Germany, would have been obvious. Professions could have been plain for all to see as craftsmen carried the tools of their trade with them to new settlements. Likewise, the sun-tanned farmer or the brawny blacksmith would have been easily distinguished from the store clerk.

While few northerners were abolitionists, and not all southerners supported slavery, such labels would have been assumed and people were treated accordingly. One might not have had time to explain the details of their political views before being assaulted.

Nothing would have occurred in secret. For example, most newspapers of the day were organs for a political party or agenda. When items arrived at the post office (there was no home delivery of mail), the community would have known the kind of newspaper read by their neighbors, where their friends and relatives lived and what kind of packages they received.

Even votes were not private. When voters reached the polls in Kansas, the ballot of a certain color indicated the candidate. Everyone would have known how their neighbors voted and made no apologies for holding them accountable.

James Stewart of New Castle, Pennsylvania, was fortunate to settle with neighbors of similar views, but the disorganization of the Western Pennsylvania Kansas Company created inconveniences for its members. About two hundred anxious settlers arrived in Kansas City, Missouri, on November 9, 1854, but the group quickly splintered because of the poor planning on the part of the organization.

This resulted in the group being divided between towns already established, with some returning to Pennsylvania. Only a handful were left to found "Council City," the town site they had selected on the Santa Fe Trail about 140 miles inside the territory. In one of many examples of poor reconnaissance, they discovered upon arriving in Kansas that their chosen site was not available for settlement because it was on the Kaw Indian Reservation. The Pennsylvanians backed up and located their Council City near the intersection of Dragoon and Switzler Creeks (present-day Burlingame). Their settlement included folks from Iowa, Ohio, New York and Indiana.

Many of those early settlers boasted of how they would take over Kansas for their cause, but few really believed that it would become a battlefield. They thought that numbers at the polling places would triumph, and thus they went about building real homes, planting crops and laying out towns—doing all the things that would establish permanent settlements instead of boomtowns.

No matter the political persuasion, Kansas was founded by people who loved government. Everybody wanted one. If it wasn't the state government, it was a local government, a militia unit or a school board—something that would lend order to society. It would appear that Kansans value order and process.

James Stewart was typical of those early, diligent settlers and was dutiful in attending to the affairs of the neighborhood. His accounts reveal that not much has changed when it comes to politics. He recorded in his diary in 1855, "The settlers meeting was of no account, had no object in view & did nothing."

Stewart's diary also reveals a camaraderie among the settlers who depended on one another for real necessities—such as trading for salt, the baking of bread, the use of oxen and sharpening tools—as well as the emotional needs. The community became family for one another, as is evident in this entry from August 1855:

> *Sat 18…Stoped and stayed all night to set up With Geo. Young Who Was very low with fever, he died between 9 & 10 O Clock, helped to dress him & sat up balance of the night.*

> *Sun 19…Dressed and went down to attend the funeral, heard the Rev. Lowry preach a funeral sermon, came home past Hovvers & got a Loaf of bread, Youngs funeral was the first I ever attended in Kansas.*

But it was far from being the last. By the end of that same month, Stewart's brother also lay dying:

> *Wed 29…Clear and beautiful all day. Went down to Freels in the morning and got his horses & Plumbs waggon and went up to Youngs cabin…after Brother Will, brought him down to my house and waited on him through the day, went down to the store in the evening and got some wine & Peruvian bark, also some milk at Freels, came home, got Will Smith to stay with me, am going to set up with Brother to-night, he is very bad. The Dr thinks he will not live, he called to see him to-day.*

> *Thur 30…Warm in the morning, a light shower about noon, clear in the evening…Got a chicken for Will, thence to Hoovers, got some bread, thence home, worked about the house waiting on William…Will died about half*

past eleven Oclock, sent Will Smith to help to dress him. Mr Hoover and Jim Bothel came & attended to it. Smith went to see about getting a coffin made, grave dug & shroud made, Mr Hoover remained with [me] until towards evening & then went home, Smith came back soon after and also Jim Bothel about dark. Am setting up to-night with my last Brother for the last time. What luck is to be meted out to me?

FRI 31…Clear & warm all day. Dressed up in the morning and prepared for Wills funeral, which was to occur at eleven Oclock but on account of detention in making the coffin, did not occur until about five in the evening, consequently did not get through 'till after dark, went down to Mr Brattons after the funeral and stayed there all night.

While death was close to everyone in the nineteenth century, the roughness of pioneer life brought it even nearer. In the absence of a funeral parlor, family and friends were called on to prepare the body for burial, build the coffin and dig a grave. One can see how the sharing of these tribulations bound communities together. It is all too easy to look back and think that those people were better or stronger than we are today. To believe that is to do them a discredit. They got just as cold, just as lonely, just as impatient, just as excited and just as brokenhearted. They feared the future just as we do. They had dreams. They became weary:

Lay awake all last night building air castles. Took a resolution to assume new vigor in the prosecution of worldly schemes, and in obedience to this resolution I got up very early and immediately proceeded to the garden, and worked there till the sun was about half an hour high, returned to the house, eat breakfast and started out to make one hundred rails, worked about two hours when getting dry I went to the house & Frank Smith calling in about that time, and after talking with him a short time the fever of doing big days work left me.

Stewart wrote of being blue some days and sometimes wished he were back in Pennsylvania. He wrote of finding a woman to share his life. He did go back to New Castle and take a bride, but Kansas would be his home, and it would bring him challenges beyond what he had already endured.[39]

Chapter 6

Government

The Kansas-Nebraska Act called for the temporary capital to be located at Fort Leavenworth, in the northeast corner of the Kansas Territory. Founded in 1827 near the ruins of French outpost Fort de Cavignal, Fort Leavenworth was one of a chain of forts designed to keep mostly displaced Indians and settlers away from one another. This became especially problematic along the trails to Santa Fe, Oregon and California, when thousands of Americans traveled across the Great Plains. Leavenworth in 1854 was the site of the largest federal presence in Kansas and would have had buildings that could be appropriated for use by the fledgling government.

It was three weeks after the historic act was signed before a chief executive was named. President Pierce nominated Andrew Reeder, a prominent attorney from Pennsylvania, to be the first of a long line of ill-fated, and mostly ineffective, territorial governors. The Senate Committee on Territories (conveniently chaired by Stephen Douglas) affirmed the nomination, and Reeder was sworn in on July 7.

Reeder, forty-seven, had never held public office, but he had a prominent law practice and was a supporter of Senator Douglas. His first actions upon taking the oath were to return to Easton, Pennsylvania, to try a couple of cases and prepare his extensive practice for an extended absence. He left Pennsylvania with the fate of his law practice weighing heavily on his mind.

Reeder was greeted at Leavenworth with a formal military salute, and he addressed his constituents in the manner of a learned lawyer: "First of all, Kansas must, and with God's help it shall be, a country of law and order."

When questioned about ruffianism, Reeder responded, "So far as it shall come within my province to deal with this spirit, I pledge you that I will crush it out or sacrifice myself in the effort."[40]

With the stabbing of Isaac Cody having occurred only weeks before, ruffianism was fresh on the minds of the inhabitants of the fledgling town of Leavenworth, built just four miles south of the fort. Since this was a predominantly proslavery area, there may have been differing opinions as to exactly which side was composed of ruffians.

Reeder may have had good intentions, but the difficulties of managing the far-flung populace of the territory soon became apparent. One of his first duties was to hold an election to elect a congressman. This required establishing districts, taking a census, appointing polling places and listing eligible voters. The chief executive was eager to accomplish the tasks and familiarize himself with the geography and general condition of his new charge.

"In a very few days I discovered that the procurement of this knowledge, in consequence of the newness of the population, was utterly impossible," lamented Reeder. "I found that, unlike most new Territories, the settlements of which cluster along a single line, the small population of Kansas was sparsely distributed over a surface of about 20,000 square miles."[41]

His visits were welcomed by solicitous settlers, all of whom wanted him to select their site for the permanent capital. Desiring to make as good an impression as possible, the good citizens of Lawrence sent to Missouri for a squash and made squash pies. This must have been an unpleasant piece of commerce, as it drove home the bitter truth that long-established Missouri possessed many things the territory did not.

The good people of Lawrence made as proper a meal as they could, charging one dollar each for the privilege of dining with the governor in the hay tent, which alternately served as a boardinghouse or a church. S.C. Pomeroy, of the Emigrant Aid Society, climbed atop an overturned box and welcomed the dignitaries, stating the glaringly obvious: "Our treasures, as you see, are little else than our true hearts and free hands."

The truthfulness of these words was underscored by the speaker's appearance. "Pomeroy was dressed in coarse, plain cloth. Hiss [sic] fur cap was quite weatherbeaten and seedy, his face well tanned by exposure to our trying winds and sun," wrote Joseph Savage. "His hair long, and lay in mattered curls about his neck."[42]

Whatever the material circumstances, a visit from the governor lent credibility and offered hope to struggling settlers. Cyrus K. Holliday wrote of the executive's visit to Topeka when it was just days old. "Governor Reeder passed through our place the day before yesterday and spoke very encouragingly of our enterprise," Holliday said to his wife. "We hope all will go well."[43]

The well-intentioned Reeder soon strayed from his path of public service and was removed from office. President Franklin Pierce noted:

> *The governor, instead of exercising constant vigilance and putting forth all his energies to prevent or counteract the tendencies to illegality which are prone to exist in all imperfectly organized and newly associated communities, allowed his attention to be diverted from official obligations by other objects, and himself set an example of the violation of law in the performance of acts which rendered it my duty in the sequel to remove him from the office of chief executive magistrate of the Territory.*

Apparently, while the governor and members of his cabinet were on their fact-finding mission, they took advantage of the many opportunities for speculation as well as the loosely formed government.

"Reeder and his colleagues, attempted," wrote one historian, "apparently illegally, to purchase the land of the half-breed Kansas Indians located north of the Kansas River…Reeder also tried, by means of an unauthorized survey which diminished the area of the military reservation, to make provision for the projected town of Pawnee, which he later designated the territorial capital."[44] Even though these schemes may have been initiated before Reeder even arrived, he appeared to have joined in the shady deals. Thus he was removed from office but not before presiding over that first historic, and quite fraudulent, election in Kansas.

CHESS AND POLITICS

The home of Thomas and Julia Stinson was the logical voting place for the village of Tecumseh, between Lawrence and Topeka. Founded the day after Topeka, Tecumseh also had aspirations to be the capital.

Julia Stinson was born at the Shawnee Indian Mission, near present-day Kansas City. She was a cousin to Tecumseh, the well-known leader of the tribe, and a treaty with the United States gave Julia eight hundred acres of land in what would become Kansas. She met and married Thomas Stinson, of Ohio, at the mission. Thomas was an experienced merchant who had traded with the Kaws, Delawares and Potawatomis before he and Julia moved to the farm in Shawnee County. Their house was located on the highway of the day, the road that took settlers west to Oregon, California or Santa Fe.

Governor Andrew Reeder was a frequent guest at the Stinsons' since it was a convenient and safe stopover. Julia Stinson told a reporter in 1915, "He would stay here in this because it was about the only one around in this part of the country, and because the slavery men wouldn't take him in…Here in Tecumseh and over at Lecompton was the headquarters of the slavery men. They hated Governor Reeder like poison."[45]

Mrs. Stinson recalled one particular visit, at a time when the governor was fleeing the territory. "After supper the governor asked me to play a game of chess," Julia said, "like we always did when he was staying at the house. I told him I would as soon as I got the baby to sleep." They had just begun their game when they were startled to hear a mob coming toward the house. Proslavery men were camped nearby on the river and heard that the chief executive was there.

"There must have been three hundred of them," she recalled, "and everyone of them full of liquor." Julia said that they were calling out the governor's name and yelled that they wanted to ride him on a rail and kill him. Her husband went out to quiet the crowd and got nowhere. He slipped back inside the door, "white as a sheet," and suggested that his wife try. She tried logic, informing the group that Reeder couldn't help where he was born, and naturally, coming from Pennsylvania, he was a free stater. (In a twist of irony, Reeder, a Democrat, had been proslavery before becoming governor. Seeing border ruffianism firsthand had pushed him to the other side.)

Julia immediately saw that in their drunken state, there was no point in telling the mob that they could not have the governor. She tried a different tactic: flattery. "'What does a bunch of nice looking men like you want to be running around like this for?' I asked them. 'I know that gentlemen like you wouldn't do such a thing as to come in my house when I hadn't asked you.'"

After firing off their guns and their mouths, the mob quieted when Mrs. Stinson told that them they could have Reeder in the morning when he left. They agreed and made camp on the grass surrounding the Stinson home. Meanwhile, Julia told the governor to throw a shawl over himself so that in the dark he appeared to be a woman. They stepped over the snoring men and their guns and made their way to their spring. After a long, dark, tense wait, Governor Reeder's driver met them with his buggy, and the chief executive gratefully climbed in to be driven safely to Lawrence. Just before Reeder told Julia goodbye, he leaned over and whispered, "You remember how those chessmen stood, Mrs. Stinson. When this trouble's over I'm coming back to finish that game."

The next morning found Mrs. Stinson pleading for her husband's life, as the mob wanted to hang him when they searched the house and found that the governor had already left. She implored them to hurry after Reeder and leave her husband, not informing them that Reeder was hours ahead.

Reeder's adventure was not over, either. With the Kansas Territory so unsafe, almost in the manner of the Underground Railroad that helped slaves escape to freedom, a series of supporters aided the governor in escaping the perils of the territory. For the last leg of his journey, the prominent man disguised himself as a woodcutter.

During that first territorial election, the voting at the Stinson home was not as exciting as other events or the balloting at other locations. It was later determined that 1,114 "legal" votes were cast (including the 48 cast at Tecumseh), as well as 1,729 "illegal" votes, mostly by Missourians who came over to vote and then went home. The proslavery candidate, obviously, carried the day—John W. Whitfield, late of Missouri, was elected as the delegate to Congress.

The next election was held in March 1855 to elect a legislature. Those results took fraud to whole new levels. There were more than six thousand votes cast but only about three thousand eligible voters in the territory. The governor recognized the legislature's right to meet, but he thought that the legislature should meet farther from Missouri to avoid the influence of the proslavery faction. He convened the legislature at Pawnee, near Fort Riley, on July 2, 1855. (Reeder's motives were called into question when the public realized that he had a considerable real estate investment at Pawnee.)

During their brief meeting, the legislators enacted laws protecting slavery in Kansas. These laws instituted the death penalty for helping a slave run away from his or her owner, and voting and jury service depended on one's willingness to return escaped slaves. Speaking or writing a statement challenging the right to own slaves was punishable by two years in prison. The legislature also organized and named counties, honoring many proslavery leaders. They also voted to move away from this backwater and back to Shawnee Mission. This legislative event was nicknamed the "bogus legislature" because of the voter fraud involved in the elections.

President Pierce flatly stated that had Reeder reached the territory sooner and gotten the census underway and generally provided stability and order, things would have turned out differently. In the grand scheme of things, Whitfield did not have a lot of power as a representative, and his election was not exactly meaningless, but it was close. As historian Russell Hickman pointed out, these first elections demonstrated Reeder's inability to manage the territory, as well as the determination of Missouri to claim Kansas as its own.[46] The mismanagement of the electoral process provided the justification for opponents, free staters, to hold their own elections, and though they may have held the moral high ground as to the slavery issue, their obvious refusal to accept the results of the political process put them on shaky ground. Although one might be sympathetic to their cause and understanding of their frustration, the elections held by free staters had no legal authority.

Wilson Shannon was named as the next territorial governor. Governor Reeder, however, did eventually return to Kansas and joined the free state efforts.

The Kansas Territory was a political mess.

Chapter 7

The Wakarusa War

In November 1855, Franklin Coleman shot Charles Dow and killed him. Had this occurred in any place other than Kansas, at any time other than November 1855, it would have been a straightforward murder with a simple trial and a just resolution. But it did occur in Kansas in 1855, and the politics of the time changed everything.

Dow was a free state man. Coleman was a proslaver. Coleman was not arrested, and Dow's neighbors were understandably upset. Jacob Branson, with whom Dow lived, rallied the community and called for action. However, the proslavery folks acted first. In one of the most ludicrous turn of events during the territorial period, Branson was arrested for talking about the fact that Coleman should be arrested. Such were the laws of the bogus legislature.

Sheriff Sam Jones, a legitimate officer of the law even though he represented the proslavery faction, brought a posse of about twenty men to Branson's home one cold midnight and took him away to jail. His wife stood in the doorway, watching until they were out of sight, fully believing that her husband was about to be killed. As the word spread throughout the community, Branson's supporters also began to gather. They went from house to house, dragging other free state men from their warm beds and into the cold night to save Branson's life. Though many of these men came from the countryside around Wakarusa, Sam Wood and a few other men from Lawrence joined them. Wood was one of the original settlers of Lawrence and a staunch abolitionist. They guessed the path that Sheriff Jones would be taking to the jail and waited for the party at

James Abbott's house. Many of the men went inside to get warm, leaving others to keep watch. One of those was a mere child, Charles Dickson. He was the first to see the posse and alerted the rescuers.[47]

Sheriff Jones could make out a group of men in the road and asked what they were up to. They responded by asking him a question, "Is Branson there?"

Branson himself shouted the answer, "I'm here!"

The rescuers told Branson to ride forward, but the posse told him that they would shoot him if he did. Branson kicked the mule he was riding to goad him forward and joined his friends, all the time fearing that he would be shot in the back. Both groups were armed to the teeth. Being so evenly matched, it was a standoff. Branson was returned to his home, but not before the sheriff shouted to Sam Wood, one of the only men he recognized, "You'll be sorry!" The sheriff vowed to return to rearrest Branson, as well as Wood, and he sent word to Territorial Governor Wilson Shannon that he needed reinforcements. Shannon issued a proclamation calling out the Kansas militia, which really meant the ruffians from Missouri.[48]

Sam Wood was one of the first settlers in Lawrence and one of the strongest proponents for a free state of Kansas. He was present at the rescue of Jacob Branson that precipitated the Wakarusa War. *Kansas State Historical Society.*

This was the beginning of the short-lived Wakarusa War. Bracing for the return of Sheriff Jones and his small army of mostly Missourians, the citizens of Lawrence organized a committee of safety that selected Dr. Charles Robinson to command the defenders, with James H. Lane second in command. Any of the men involved in the rescue of Jacob Branson were instructed to leave town, thereby removing any legitimate cause for a raid on the citizens. The town was fortified by throwing up earthworks at the entrances. (Lieutenant Colonel Phillip St. George Cooke, stationed at Fort Leavenworth, was decidedly unimpressed when he saw the fortifications that the townspeople had built.) They formed units of fifteen to twenty men and drilled constantly. Members of Sheriff Jones's "posse" were camping at nearby Franklin and at Lecompton. Among the Missourians joining the fray was U.S. Senator David Rice Atchison, as the distinctions between political and military power blurred so often on the border.

Men came from surrounding communities to aid in the defense. One of those was Thomas Barber. On December 6, 1855, Barber was killed, most likely by George Clark. Barber had been riding with his brother and another gentleman when they happened upon a proslavery group, among them Indian agent George Clark. This may have been one of those incidents that boiled down to just being in the wrong place at the wrong time. Whatever the cause, Barber was killed, a martyr to the cause, and his young wife was left a widow. His slayer bragged that he had sent one more "damned abolitionist to his winter quarters."[49]

Barber's murder inspired John Greenleaf Whittier to pen yet another poem, and soon the "Burial of Barber" became a rallying cry for the free state cause:

Bear him, comrades, to his grave;
Never over one more brave
Shall the prairie grasses weep…
…And above the broken sod,
Once again, to Freedom's God,
Pledge ourselves for life or death.
That the State whose walls we lay,
In our blood and tears, to-day,
Shall be free from bonds of shame,
And our goodly land untrod
By the feet of Slavery, shod
With cursing as with flame!
Plant the Buckeye on his grave,
For the hunter of the slave
In its shadow cannot rest;
And let martyr mound and tree
Be our pledge and guaranty
Of the freedom of the West![50]

Territorial Governor Wilson Shannon also served as the governor of Ohio and minister to Mexico prior to the Mexican-American War. His older brother, George, was a member of the Lewis and Clark expedition. Unable to control the situation in Kansas, he fled the territory in 1856 but returned after statehood and practiced law in Lawrence. *Kansas State Historical Society.*

When Governor Wilson Shannon arrived, he brokered a peace, of sorts, in the weeklong war. Historian Frank W. Blackmar described the affair:

> *It was a strange spectacle, almost a comedy had it not been so near a tragedy, and in any case was certainly a travesty on free government, for the United States Senator Atchison to be commanding this singular horde, while Gov. Shannon was hurrying other commands to the scene of war. There was no excuse for it all…here was another scene in the drama of spectacular government; the town of Lawrence in rebellion, treating with the Kansas militia, the latter commanded by officers living in Missouri.*[51]

Chapter 8

Same Song, Second Verse

E verything except grudges froze in the Kansas Territory during the winter of 1855–56. While residents huddled together, trying to survive subzero temperatures in lean-tos and crude cabins, resentments festered and revenge flourished in fireside conversations. Come spring, there would be retribution.

The Wakarusa War dissolved into one of words rather than altercations after the killing of Thomas Barber and the peace negotiated by Territorial Governor Wilson Shannon. But the winter had given the factions time to plan, time for news of various depredations to spread and time to recruit more and more men to fight. From mere appearances, it would have been difficult to know which side was which since there were no uniforms for these home guards, posses or militia groups. A news correspondent described one of these men, the legendary proslavery sheriff:

> *Sheriff Jones is a tall, rather good-looking man, with a profusion of light auburn hair over his face, and a curious habit of shutting up his left eye when in conversation, which gives an appearance of cunning to an otherwise bold, and frank seeming countenance. He, like all the territorial officials I have seen, was emphatically seedy in his dress, though this may likewise be remarked of our Free State men, whose lack of good clothes arises, not so much from carelessness as from the poverty that environs them.*[52]

Indeed, stylish clothing and personal grooming were luxuries on the Kansas frontier, for survival (politically and physically) consumed all energy. Cyrus K. Holliday wrote of their circumstances, "Our washing we get done as we can—For myself I am wearing to day a shirt that I put on two weeks ago and scarcely know when I will get a clean one. But this is all right... Clean shirts & good living will come after awhile and then our territory will far eclipse anything you can find in the East."[53]

James Stewart, a Pennsylvanian in Osage County, found his days consumed by chores. The occasional political meeting in those early days served to remind him of why he had come to Kansas and was enduring such hardships. There were meetings to form literary societies and governing bodies, as well as meetings of stockholders in this and that association, as the good pioneers established communities with hopes of their growing into thriving towns. Public discussions debated the issues of the day, from slavery to women's suffrage. But the day-to-day living was often lonely and sometimes dull:

> *Sun 10—Clear and beautiful, a good breeze. Killed a rattle-snake in the house this morning, wrote a letter...*

> *Mon 11—Warm and pleasant. Made rails, read, fiddled, rested, done nothing, built air castles had big notions of getting a woman, and played hell generally*

> *Tues 12—Rained more or less all day. Made a few rails, read history, went down town, bought some flour, took it over to Hoovers, thence to the boarding house, returned home, got as wet as possible going through the long grass.*

> *Wed 13—Pleasant all day. Made a few rails, read some worked in the garden, pulled some radishes, took them down to Mrs Hoover, got some bread, returned home.*[54]

Except for the occasional confrontation with a poisonous snake or a death in the community, Stewart's diary is much the same every day. Rarely are the boredom and drudgery of pioneer life mentioned as contributing factors to violence, but they most assuredly were. It was certainly a factor that pushed politics to the center of their lives. It was entertainment. Historian Harold Holzer described the atmosphere of the Lincoln-Douglas debates, and this would have been true of most political gatherings of the time:

> *With little to entertain them outside church and county fairs, Americans flocked by the thousands to political events. Spectators stood for hours, toted banners, hocked wares, fired cannons, downed hard drink and raucously interrupted speakers with hurrahs and harassment—there was no Brian Williams–like proscription against audience response.*
>
> *It was not uncommon for fistfights to break out in the farthest reaches of these large crowds, where the unamplified voices of the debaters seldom reached. During one debate, a Republican smeared excrement on Douglas's carriage. Such diversions helped audiences endure outdoor marathons at which the opening speaker held forth for an hour, the responder took 90 minutes, and the first debater topped off with a half-hour rejoinder—unthinkable in today's sound-bite culture.*[55]

This was especially true in Kansas, and once again, the state had its own set of special circumstances within nineteenth-century culture. The old saying "All politics is local" especially rang true in the Kansas Territory, and it did present an urgency not known in the nation since the ratification of the Constitution. In fact, historian William Wagnon has referred to the Civil War, with its roots in Territorial Kansas, as the "second birth of freedom."[56]

GETTING THROUGH MISSOURI

It is difficult to picture how little there was for those early white settlers coming to the Kansas Territory. While the tendency is to lump everyone who lived through the 1800s into one pioneer lifestyle, that is not accurate. Farmers would have certainly been at an advantage when placed on the frontier, and townspeople would have been challenged. Most of them had come from comfortable surroundings, most had never cooked over an open fire and most had been surrounded by the homes or farms of family and friends. In settling Kansas, they left all of this behind, and it would take months and years for communities to grow to a size that would supply the comforts for which they longed.

Something as simple as an apple became infused with political meaning. There were no orchards in the territory. How long does it take an orchard to produce fruit? Where was the closest place to buy apples? Missouri. What about all those items—needles, thread, buttons, tools, cloth and canned goods—that had to be shipped through Missouri? Mail came through Missouri. News came through Missouri. There was no part of daily life in the Kansas Territory in which Missouri was not involved, which meant anything from pilfering to filtering. If items made it through Missouri, they might not be intact. From a letter Cyrus K. Holliday wrote to his wife, "I can send you no papers from Kansas—We have but two published here and they never get through Missouri."[57]

The main artery through the "Show Me State" was the Missouri River. It is difficult to imagine the number of steamboats paddling up and downstream. While the typical pioneer is pictured on a Conestoga wagon, that same pioneer would likely have been a steamboat passenger for a great deal of the journey before purchasing a wagon in western Missouri. The importance of the commerce along the river is underlined by the discovery of the wreck of the *Arabia*. The boat sank in September 1856, laden with *everything* necessary to carve a civilized life from the frontier, including perfume and Wedgwood china, locks, door handles, saws and augurs. Only months before, the boat had been boarded when a stash of carbines bound for the Kansas Territory was found on board.[58]

Steamboats were easy pickings as they maneuvered up the Missouri River. The boats moved fairly slowly, they were rarely well protected and they were full of goods. Proslavery vigilantes boarded the ships and took the supplies bound for antislavery towns or persons, while allowing those of proslavery settlers to pass. This eventually hampered communication and effectively cut off supplies between free state settlers and their supporters in the East. Some communities faced the very real prospect of starvation. At the same time, the storehouses of proslavery towns were bursting at the seams. Historian William Wagnon wrote:

> The disparities tempted desperate settlers to take matters into their own hands. In addition to building a fortification to defend Topeka from possible attacks, men assembled to make foraging expeditions into neighboring communities to relieve their store houses of commodities needed for survival. John Ritchie, among others, led these expeditions, returning with liberated wagons filled

with goods for storage in Constitution Hall. Joseph C. Miller, whose shop was located in the Hall, took charge of distributing the booty to Topeka residents. In the meantime, Jim Lane, formerly from Indiana and leader of the Topeka Free State movement, opened an overland trail that connected Topeka with the Nebraska border, where emigrants and goods could cross Iowa and enter Kansas with less hassle from the border ruffians. W.W. and Edwin [Edmund] Ross would be among the initial train to open the trail.[59]

A siege situation gripped many free state communities. In this climate, proslavery officials saw an opportunity to press the abolitionists to the wall and run them out of the territory. The catch was that free state activists had the same idea. Tensions were growing, as was the fear of an invasion from Missouri, and the mayor of Lawrence looked to the military for protection. Colonel E.V. Sumner's reply was printed in the *Lawrence Herald of Freedom*:

Head. Quar. 1ˢᵗ Cavalry
Fort Leavenworth, April 22 '56

Sir;—A small detachment proceeds to Lecompton this morning, on the requisition of the Governor, under the orders of the President, to assist the

Colonel Edwin Sumner was a cousin of the powerful Massachusetts senator Charles Sumner. The colonel had served with Jefferson Davis in the Mexican-American War, and the two remained friends until Sumner's death in 1863, despite their being on opposite sides during the war. Davis, while serving as secretary of war, handpicked his old friend to head the First U.S. Cavalry at Fort Leavenworth. *Kansas State Historical Society.*

Sheriff of Douglas County in executing several writs in which he says he has been resisted. I know nothing of the merits of the case and have nothing to do with them. But I would respectfully impress on you, and others in authority, the necessity of yielding obedience to the proclamation and orders of the General Government. Ours is emphatically a government of laws and if they are set at naught there is an end of all order. I feel assured that, on reflection you will not compel me to resort to violence in carrying out the orders of the Government.

I am sir, very respectfully,
Your obd'nt serv't

E. V. Sumner
Col. 1ˢᵗ Cavalry, Com.[60]

As a result of the rescue of Jacob Branson, warrants had been issued against some of the men involved. Judge Samuel Lecompte, in the meantime, had demanded that the free state government, organized in

The Free State Hotel in Lawrence was destroyed by cannon fire in May 1856. *Kansas State Historical Society.*

October and having met in March, be indicted for treason. Jones meant to serve those warrants and would not be disappointed if the arrests were less than peaceful. While attempting to serve these warrants in April, Sheriff Sam Jones was shot. The official was seriously wounded and reported dead. Missourians were outraged. This was an example of the "law and order" the free state government advocated, shooting a public official in the exercise of his duty? As for the sheriff, recuperating only gave him more time for feelings of revenge to fester.

So, vested with the authority of federal government and emboldened by revenge, Sheriff Jones gathered a posse (actually an army of about eight hundred men bolstered by Missouri ruffians) to destroy his old enemy Sam Wood and the rest of Lawrence along with him.

As word of the impending attack spread, free state militias from around the territory came to the aid of Lawrence. John Brown arrived from Osawatomie with his sons and neighbors. (He would be called "Captain Brown" from that time.) From Topeka came the home guard organized by Daniel Horne that included John Ritchie and John Armstrong. Aside from defending Lawrence, the time spent together was a bonding experience for these men, and it resulted, according to one historian, in "adding a military network to the political one that had created the Topeka Constitution earlier in the fall."[61]

Within Lawrence, Dr. Charles Robinson and James H. Lane were made "generals" of the free state defenders. Lane led the townspeople to build earthen fortifications. Having served in the army during the Mexican-American War, Lane had some military experience, and he drilled willing townsmen in preparation for attack. More than military ability, Lane possessed that intangible quality that enabled him to motivate others. That rare quality would have a lasting impact on the fight for Kansas.

"The Kansas war was at its height," reported G. Douglas Brewerton. "[T]he Wakarusa and Lecompton camps teemed with those barbarous hordes, the 'Border Ruffians,' when it was suddenly discovered by the stern Republicans...Who guarded the entrenchments of this beleaguered city, that our gallant defenders lacked that *sine qua non* for legalized bloodshed, powder and ball."[62] Where the men exhausted "their ingenuity in vain, a woman's wit will often solve the problem," added Brewerton.

Mrs. George W. Brown, wife of the newspaperman, believed that she would be allowed through the enemy cordon that surrounded the city. Sam

James H. Lane, a former congressman from Indiana, became a leader of the Republican Party in Kansas and the state's most colorful politician. *Kansas State Historical Society.*

Wood's wife volunteered to go with her. Mrs. Wood described the adventure to Brewerton, leaving out proper names fearing for their safety should the conversation be overheard:

> *We were both, I can assure you, got up, so far as equipments were concerned, in a very eccentric fashion for the trip; as for myself, I wore two dresses, and a petticoat, which, though it went forth lined with wadding, came back charged with what—if I were inclined to make a pun, might be called excellent gun-cotton…We passed the picket guards of the Lawrence camp, and continued on…The fact of our being females, and our traveling from the town, was probably a sufficient guarantee for our harmlessness…we reached the dwelling of Mr. Blank, our first stopping-place upon the Santa Fe trail. Here we received a warm welcome…and, what was more to the purpose, a keg of prime rifle-powder, which I should say, for I carried it out to the buggy myself, must have contained upwards of twenty-five pounds; this we emptied and secreted carefully about our persons, I could hardly*

tell you where. In addition to the powder, they gave us a quantity of lead; this we also stowed away in a secret hiding place—as for the Sharpe's rifle caps, we put those in our stockings, while the cartridges were quilted into our petticoats, under-dress, and clothing generally.[63]

The ladies continued to a second home on the Santa Fe Trail and received more supplies than they could hide, being already "*loaded* quite up to the muzzle." They had no choice but to entrust the remainder to "a sturdy Free State youngster, who although he was not yet nine years old, was going to try to enter Lawrence…with the ox team he was driving."[64]

The lad was Charles Dickson, the same brave young man who had been present at the rescue of Jacob Branson. He followed the women back to Lawrence at a distance. As they were returning to town, the women observed a camp of Missourians.

"There, sure enough, were a party of 'Border Ruffians' on horseback," recalled Mrs. Wood, "whose dark figures stood out in bold relief against the wintry sky, as they dotted the summit of a distant prairie rise, where they seemed to have reined in their cattle to observe us; while worst of all, two of their number…were already galloping towards us at top speed, as if to cut us off."[65]

The women quickly decided that there was no way of escaping except to appear innocent. Mrs. Brown continued:

Judge, then, how great was my relief, when I beheld the two horsemen, who had by this time galloped up to within twenty or thirty yards of our vehicle, tighten their bridles, and come to a sudden halt; at the same time, lifting their hats, as they assured me, with a very killing bow, that they really begged our pardon for disturbing us, which had their people only known that none but ladies were in the buggy, would never have occurred.[66]

Shortly after, young Charles, his pockets bulging with lead and driving a team of oxen, encountered the guards. He feigned silliness when interrogated and was soon dismissed as a foolish boy.[67] Then the citizens of Lawrence decided not to resist. Jones and his followers would not be cheated out of their revenge, however, and they proceeded to destroy much of the town. The newspapers were primary targets. The *Kansas Free State* and the *Herald of Freedom* were anything but objective in their reporting but rather were typical of the nineteenth century, when most newspapers openly supported one party or the other and were vital in fanning the flames of political fervor. Proslavery forces delighted in throwing the type and presses into the river. Homes and shops were also looted and burned. The Free State Hotel, a frequent meeting place for abolitionists and a symbol of the free state cause, was smashed by cannon fire.

While this might have satisfied the bloodlust of Jones and others, the repercussions were swift. The act of destroying Lawrence fueled abolitionist propaganda machines. It was the perfect piece of galvanizing news for the newspapers in the Northeast and the politicians in Washington. The situation in Kansas had obviously deteriorated, and the territory was in a state of war.

For John Brown, the impact of the attack on Lawrence was far more than a public relations coup. It pushed him over the edge. Then word arrived from the nation's capital that the abolitionist senator Charles Sumner had been physically beaten with a cane by Congressman Preston Brooks of South Carolina while Sumner had been sitting in his chair in the U.S. Senate chambers.

Something snapped inside of Old Osawatomie. Three nights later, on May 24, James and Mahala Doyle, along with their three sons, tended to their chores and went to bed. The Doyles had come from Tennessee to settle in what they hoped would be the fertile and prosperous Kansas Territory. They had been in the territory only six months.

"At the midnight hour, noise outside their Pottawattomie Creek homestead awoke the family. Banging on their door, angry men drew James P. Doyle from his bed along with William and Drury, the couple's eldest sons," wrote historian Michelle Martin. "Without warning, the band of marauders marched the three Doyles two hundred yards and killed them where they stood. This night would become infamous in the pages of history. On this black night, John Brown had come bringing death and desolation."[68]

Two other settlers, Allen Wilkinson and William Sherman, were dragged from their homes and killed. Mahala would later testify that soon after her husband and boys were taken from the home, she heard the reports of a pistol and then moaning. Her son, John Doyle, later offered this horrific testimony on the affair:

> *The next morning was Sunday, the 25th of May, 1856. I went in search*
> *of my father and two brothers. I found my father and one brother, William,*

lying dead in the road, about two hundred yards from the house; I saw my other brother lying dead on the ground, about one hundred and fifty yards from the house, in the grass, near a ravine; his fingers were cut off; and his arms were cut off; his head was cut open; there was a hole in his breast. William's head was cut open, and a hole was in his jaw, as though it was made by a knife, and a hole was also in his side. My father was shot in the forehead and stabbed in the breast.[69]

Testimony from their neighbors was just as gruesome. James Harris described how Old Man Brown and his men came into their one-room cabin, ransacked it and asked for bridles, saddles and information on other settlers. When William Sherman was taken outside, he did not return. James Harris noted:

That morning about ten o'clock I found William Sherman dead in the creek near my house. I was looking for Mr. Sherman, as he had not come back, I thought he had been murdered. I took Mr. William Sherman out of the creek and examined him. Mr. Whiteman was with me. Sherman's skull was split open in two places and some of his brains was washed out by the water. A large hole was cut in his breast, and his left hand was cut off except a little piece of skin on one side. We buried him.[70]

If Brown's intentions were to create a state of panic and terror, he succeeded. The families of the victims moved away, as did many of their neighbors. Then came June.

Chapter 9

Black Jack

T here was no need for propaganda. The facts coming from Kansas had become so incredible that no embellishment was necessary. Brown had transformed from an antislavery activist to the avenging angel of the Lord. Any thought of building homes or planting crops was entirely gone, and mere words and politics were not enough. Violence was the only way to rid Kansas of slavery and those who would support it. John Brown's holy war had begun.

News of the massacre spread beyond the Kansas/Missouri border and shocked the nation, further driving a wedge into the regional divisions and further inflaming the proslavery forces in Missouri who swept into the Kansas Territory to capture Brown and bring him to justice. One of these groups, led by Captain Henry Clay Pate, encountered John Brown on the Santa Fe Trail a short distance from Baldwin City.

"After looting the near-by free state town of Palmyra, Pate's posse settled into camp here along the Santa Fe Trail near a post office called Black Jack," wrote one historian. "The following dawn, June 2, 1856, the 25 men in Pate's command were rudely awakened by the song of whistling balls. So intent on catching Old Brown was Pate, that he never imagined Old Brown might catch him."[71]

Pate had camped in the perfect trap—in the low, shaded ground next to the creek with high prairies rising on either side. Not fully understanding the nature of Brown, he had never considered taking a defensive position and logically chose the site that offered him firewood and water. All he and his men could do upon waking to the attack was seek cover behind their wagons and fire back. Brown, realizing that he had the advantage of surprise, ran down the hill closer and stooped for protection in the ruts of the trail. Looking around, he realized that many of his forty men had deserted, leaving Brown the one who was outnumbered. Pate, of course, did not know this.

For three hours, the two sides shot at each other, and then Brown's son, Frederick, who was mentally a little slow, appeared behind Pate's men, waving a sword and shouting, "Father, we have them surrounded!" Brown ordered his remaining men to shoot at the horses and mules instead of the men—all of these circumstances were unnerving for the southerners. White flags began to appear from the woods.

A cold chill must have gone down Pate's spine when the two sides came face to face, and he realized that he had surrendered to Old Osawatomie, who only days before had butchered five men. But Pate and the other captives were treated considerately. Their wounds were cared for, and they were well fed.

The Peacekeeper

Colonel E.V. Sumner, U.S. Cavalry, could not have had a more exasperating assignment than that of keeping the peace in the Kansas Territory. The constant "tattling" by both sides would have been humorous had the stakes not been so high. While many decried him as a coward or accused the officer of supporting the other side, neither of these was true. Sumner was simply a dutiful and diligent soldier. His response to the mayor of Lawrence in April when asked to intervene in affairs there demonstrated Sumner's view of the soldier's role in following orders without prejudice, as well as his fervent belief in the American process.

Nicknamed "Bull" for his booming voice, he left little doubt who was in charge when he was present. On March 3, 1855, Sumner was promoted to colonel and handpicked by Secretary of War Jefferson Davis to head an elite cavalry unit being formed at Fort Leavenworth. Davis and Sumner were old friends; they had served together in the Mexican-American War, and their paths would cross again and again.

March 3 was the same day Lieutenant James Ewell Brown Stuart was transferred to the fort after duty in Texas. Only a few years past graduating from West Point, the young Virginian was an accomplished horseman and an extremely capable manager. Where Sumner was strident, Stuart was daring. Stuart, who was bright and ambitious, often shook his head over the demands of his senior officer, and Sumner could be unbending, but that was, and is, not an unusual situation in the army. They occasionally grated on each other, but they actually formed an effective team.

When word of the events at Black Jack reached the combat veteran, Sumner reacted as he always did: he would follow his orders, nothing more, not a wit less. He represented the authority of the United States government, and he would use every resource available to him to carry out his duty. He was known as a man of his word. His orders were straightforward and simple: relieve John Brown of his prisoners. There was no mention of arresting Brown or any of his followers, and Sumner would not take it upon himself to make policy. Sumner's command found Brown's party on the Santa Fe Trail, that superhighway of the territorial years. Pate and his associates were rescued without incident, but of greater significance that day was the fact that Lieutenant Stuart and John Brown met face to face. This encounter would have historic consequences in the years to follow.

INDEPENDENCE DAY

Terror had spread through the Kansas Territory. In the wake of the sack of Lawrence, just shy of thirty miles to the west, Topekans feared for their safety. Residents begged Colonel Sumner to come to their aid, fearing the growing lawless state that existed throughout the territory. "The same band of armed and lawless men are threatening the peaceably disposed citizens of Topeka with death, and their city with total destruction," Topekans wrote. "From the recent unprovoked attack upon Lawrence, the undersigned greatly fear their said threat may be carried into execution."[72]

Sumner did not come. He had no orders and would not move without them.

Some settlers decided that staying just wasn't worth the risk and went home. Others had invested every dime they had into this country and could not afford to change their minds. Still others were committed to the cause and determined to stay for that reason. One of those was Cyrus K. Holliday. He wrote from Topeka in mid-June:

My Dear Wife—

I wrote you last on last Sunday. While many things have transpired during the past week yet they have been of such a public and notorious character that you will obtain a better account of them through the public prints than I could possibly write them...I wrote to you on the 1st day of June not to come to Kansas until you could hear from me again. Since then I wrote to you twice, I think, repeating the same, and I now repeat again. You & Mr Nichols must not start until I tell you to come. I think matters will take a more favorable turn in a few days weeks at most. Yesterday—Sunday—The Ft. Riley Troops—Cannon and all, passed through this place on their way to the scene of Strife—The Ft. Leavenworth troops have been in the field for some time. We are hourly expecting word if a sanguinary battle between the U.S. Troops and the Border Ruffians—There will be about 1000 on a side—with Cannon, Dragoons, Infantry &c. &c. upon each side and it will be a desperate battle—Look out for the news of the result—Should there be a fight there is no telling when the thing will end.[73]

The free state legislature was to convene in Topeka on July 4. Free state leaders had also called for a convention of believers to also gather in support of the delegates. Among the delegates was Isaac Cody, who had brought his son, Willie, with him for the historic event. He had been elected by his free state brethren at Grasshopper Falls. Isaac was as involved as possible in the free state cause, although he had not fully recovered from the wounds he had received when he was stabbed in 1854.

The anything-but-objective journalist James Redpath reported that as many as eight hundred men had gathered by July 3, and five hundred of those were well armed. Nerves were frayed by the violence of the past months. It was an incredibly hot day, political tensions were high and people had guns. Across the Kansas River to the north, a few miles away, were five companies from Fort Riley.

Colonel Sumner and five companies of cavalry from Fort Leavenworth had camped on the outskirts of Topeka on July 3. Topeka was a powder keg about to explode. Territorial Governor Wilson Shannon had begged Sumner to be there in person and not send a subordinate. "It's a matter of utmost importance that you shall be present," Shannon wrote. "You understand the whole matter, and can do more with these people than anyone else."[74]

The Topeka Constitutional Convention was one of several, as factions fought to submit their own documents to Congress for approval, all the while lobbying to make their town the new state capital. *Kansas State Historical Society.*

Colonel Sumner did understand "these people" perfectly. "From beginning to end," wrote Sumner, "I have known no party in this affair. My measures have necessarily born hard against both parties, for both have, in many instances, been more or less wrong."[75]

On the morning of July 4, a cannon salute from the cavalry encampment woke the townspeople. There were flags on the businesses and in front of every tent. Banners boasted "Our lives for our rights."

The convention began at 8:00 a.m. with speeches by various officials, including Reverend Pardee Butler of Atchison. Butler, like Cody, was an outspoken opponent to slavery in a community of differing beliefs, and like Cody, he had paid dearly for his ideals. When he had not heeded the admonitions of the proslavery men to change his rhetoric, they had taken him to the Missouri River bank, covered him with tar and feathers and set him afloat on the wide river in the hopes that he would not survive to reach dry land. But on the off chance that he would, he was instructed never to come back. His last words to his captors were, "If I drown, I'll forgive you!"[76]

Amid the inspirational speeches, Marshal Donaldson brought proclamations from everyone from the president to the acting governor to Colonel Sumner declaring that the legislative body was not allowed to meet.

"As soon as the proclamations were read the business of the convention was resumed, as if no interruption had occurred," recorded Redpath. "Marshal Donaldson remained. He looked as a countryman looks at a railroad for the first time—utterly amazed, apparently, at the conduct and coolness of the convention. He left."

The marshal went straight to Colonel Sumner and told him the meeting was proceeding. Though Redpath reported that Sumner was "excited" by the news, knowing Sumner's personality, that is difficult to believe. Irritated was probably more accurate. That he sprang into predetermined action at the words is perfectly plausible. As unpleasant as the prospect was, Colonel Sumner and many of his men were prepared and expecting to fight. James Redpath wrote:

> *Colonel Sumner, by a series of rapid movements, stationed his men, with admirable skill, in three divisions—one drawn up in front of Constitution Hall; another in line with it, but further up the street; a third several paces back and between the first and third divisions. There was no intention of resisting the United States troops; and, therefore, the Colonel could easily station his forces in the most formidable position. If the people had intended to fight him, he never would have been permitted to enter Topeka. The drummer of Company G, Topeka Guards, was beating when the troops entered town. He kept on and the company stood firm, even when the dragoons were riding toward them. The drummer plied his sticks regularly until the head of the horse of the first file touched him. He made one step forward and then stood still. So with the others; none moved till the horses of the troops could go no further without stepping on them, and then they made only one step forward and immediately "dressed left." Colonel Sumner looked at them half angrily, half admiringly. The drummer still kept on, and did not desist until requested to do so by the colonel.*[77]

Two pieces of artillery were stationed on Kansas Avenue. The "slow match," used to fire the cannon, was lit.

When Sumner dismounted to enter the government chambers, Redpath observed that he was very agitated. "The man appeared to be much ashamed of the soldier," said Redpath, possibly projecting his own ardent abolitionist values into the situation. "Colonel Sumner is a true gentleman; but the tool of Pierce, and is he not to be pitied?"[78]

As Sumner strode through the House chambers, ladies stepped up and introduced themselves. Not wishing to be rude, but obviously not having the patience for distraction, the colonel quickly took their hands then took his leave. "Ladies, I am sorry to interrupt you, but I must attend to my duty," and with that he was gone, and the ladies were talking after him.[79] The episode highlights the presence of so many civilian onlookers in the midst of soldiers and armed militia. The colonel was keenly aware of the lives in his hands that day.

The meeting was called to order and the roll of delegates called "with as much coolness and regularity as if Colonel Sumner had been at Leavenworth and Franklin Pierce a myth," wrote the correspondent. But Sumner was very much present:

> *"Gentlemen, I am called upon this day to perform the most painful duty of my life. Under the authority of the president's proclamation, I*

Colonel Edwin Sumner directs his troops, who are facing the local militia on Kansas Avenue, Topeka, July 4, 1856. The free state legislature was meeting illegally in Constitution Hall, and the president ordered Sumner to stop the meeting. *Kansas State Historical Society.*

am here to disperse the legislature, and I therefore inform you that you cannot meet. I therefore, in accordance with my orders, command you to disperse. God knows that I have no party feeling in this matter, and will have none as long as I hold my present position in Kansas. I have just returned from the borders, where I have been sending home companies of Missourians, and now I am ordered to disperse you. Such are my orders, that you must disperse."

[Judge Schuyler:] *"Are we to understand that the legislature is dispersed at the point of a bayonet?"*

[Colonel Sumner:] *"I shall use all the forces under my command to carry out my orders." Colonel Sumner then sat down and the house and audience dispersed.*[80]

Sumner made the same speech to the Senate, which likewise terminated its meeting. As he mounted his horse, the crowd gave three cheers for the colonel, indicating that they did not hold him responsible for the act he was commanded to perform. Then there were three cheers for John C. Frémont, candidate for president. Then the crowd gave three hearty groans for President Franklin Pierce. All of this occurred as a new American flag was raised over Constitution Hall.

Then came August.

Chapter 10

Insurrection

On August 25, 1856, the governor declared the Kansas Territory to be in a state of insurrection.

Would that be Governor Wilson Shannon, on his way out? Was it Daniel Woodson, the native Virginian and secretary of state who found himself acting governor four times? Or would that be John White Geary, the six-foot-six Pennsylvanian on his way to take over the chaotic conditions?

In fact, it was "acting" Governor Woodson, and it was an understatement. It was the cool-headedness and commitment to duty of Colonel Edwin Sumner that had kept full-scale civil war from breaking out in Topeka on July 4. With armed militia and an elite cavalry unit facing each other, had shots been fired there would have been no way to put the genie of war back into the bottle. The Civil War would have begun then and there, and those in rebellion would have been the antislavery forces.

However, since July, there had been skirmishes between free state and proslavery forces at Franklin, Fort Saunders, Fort Titus and Middle Creek. At Franklin, a burning hay wagon had forced proslavers to surrender their position in a barn. At Fort Saunders, David Hoyt from Massachusetts was killed. Henry Titus barely escaped execution when his proslavery stronghold was overrun. One of the free staters was mortally wounded in the attack.

Word spread of an outrageous attack at Leavenworth. A man named Fugit made a bet that he would take a Yankee scalp. He rode out into the countryside and met a German by the name of Hoppe. When he asked Hoppe if he lived in Lawrence, he replied in the affirmative; Fugit pulled his revolver and fired one fatal shot into the man's forehead. He then leaped from his horse, pulled a knife, cut the scalp from the poor man's head and tied it to a pole, proudly displaying it as he returned to Leavenworth. It was also reported that when the widow came to claim her husband's body, Fugit forced her onto a steamer and sent her back down the river.[81]

Casualties were minimal, but men were dying on both sides, and given the relatively small population of the territory, each violent death left a gaping hole in the community, as well as a growing fear that there was no end in sight.

From Lawrence and Topeka, the attention turned to Osawatomie. John Brown's sister and brother-in-law had settled there, and the notoriety Brown had brought down on himself and his family had a high price. On August 30, four hundred Missourians burned and looted the city. Brown's force of only forty defenders was no match for the superior numbers. Spencer Kellogg Brown, a young man of only fourteen, was home with his brother when they saw the enemy approaching. Their father being away in Lawrence getting supplies, it was up to the young men to take action. A shot rang out, and someone shouted, "The Missourians are coming!" Spencer's first thought was to inform his neighbors. In a short time, he found himself surrounded. He tried to remain casual:

> *I mixed freely among the Missourians talking until a man named Taggart who knew me took me prisoner.*
>
> *I will acknowledge my blood grew cold when he told me to follow him. I did not say anything however. He took me to a house where they had fourteen other prisoners…Soon they began to question me. Wanted to know how many free state men there were, and if I were Old John Brown's Son. I told them I did not know how many free state men were here, thought about 50, at the most but doubted if there were so many. They told me that I lied; that there were two hundred and fifty. I said that I was not Capt. Brown's son. Then I heard the word given to burn the town which made a very hot fire. After that they loaded the wagons with the goods plundered from the houses. One of them ordered me to put the chairs on the wagon which I did not do, wherewith he came running at me with his bayonet, cursing and threatening to "stick" me if I did not do it…*

Several of the Missourians were very badly wounded. When on their retreat from the town, they stopped at our house while they plundered and then burnt it. They attempted to get out the piano, but in the excitement and heat of the rapidly spreading flames they were compelled to drop it in the doorway, two partly burnt legs and the iron frame only remained to tell the story of its final end.[82]

Spencer said he was only half-dressed and his captors allowed him to get clothes from his home before they burned it. "I met a man with my violin which I got from him," wrote the lad, "but not without some trouble. I found two or three suits of clothes and some underwear as they had just come from the laundry and I got a pair of moccasins."

Spencer was forced to witness the plunder and destruction of his own home. Imagine his increased outrage and helplessness at seeing the family's horse being stolen: "I walked out to the road when I saw a man take our horse and made me ride her a little ways. There was a fire raging in one of the chambers when I first reached home and soon it was all in a blaze."[83]

Spencer would be a prisoner for several months. John Brown's son, Frederick, was killed, the first of his children to be sacrificed for the cause.

On September 3, Jefferson Davis requisitioned two regiments of foot militia from the governors of Kentucky and Illinois, to be assigned to General Persifor F. Smith, commanding the Department of the West. Davis also sent instructions to General Smith giving him the authority to request from Governor Geary any of the militia forces raised in the territory and transfer them to U.S. service. All these actions were necessary to "suppress insurrectionary combinations against the constituted Government of the Territory of Kansas."[84] Matters were so desperate that the chief of the Delaware nation in northeast Kansas petitioned the military for protection.[85]

All this was happening while John Geary was en route to Kansas. As he was coming up the Missouri River, who should he run into but the recently removed governor Wilson Shannon. They visited at length, and to his credit, Governor Geary still continued on to Kansas.

Geary arrived in Leavenworth on September 9. The very next day, "Governor" Robinson (elected in March by the extralegal free state legislature) was released from imprisonment on charges of treason by posting a $5,000 bail. Also released were John Brown Jr. and H.H. Williams.

First impressions are often flawed, but in the case of Governor Geary, they were precisely accurate. Hours after arriving, Geary wrote to the president:

I find that I have not simply to contend against bands of armed ruffians and brigands, whose sole aim and end is assassination and robbery; infatuated adherents and advocates of conflicting political sentiments and local institutions, and evil-disposed persons actuated by a desire to obtain elevated position, but, worst of all, against the influence of men who have been placed in authority, and have employed all the destructive agents around them to promote their own personal interests at the sacrifice of every just, honorable, and lawful consideration.

I have barely time to give you a brief statement of facts as I find them. The town of Leavenworth is now in the hands of armed bodies of men, who, having been enrolled as militia, perpetrate outrages of the most atrocious character under the shadow of authority from the Territorial Government.

Within a few days these men have robbed and driven from their homes unoffending citizens, have fired upon and killed others in their own dwellings, and stolen horses and property, under the pretense of employing them in the public service. They have seized persons who had committed no offense, and after stripping them of all their valuables, placed them on steamers and sent them out of the Territory.

In isolated or country places no man's life is safe. The roads are filled with armed robbers, and murders for mere plunder are of daily occurrence. Almost every farmhouse is deserted, and no traveler has the temerity to venture upon the highways without an escort.[86]

Not too many miles to the west of Governor Geary lay Hickory Point in Jefferson County. Geary may never have even heard of that dot on the map, but before he could unpack his belongings, it would be the location of the most important event in the territory.

Captain T.J. Wood was camped with a contingent of cavalry near Lecompton on the south side of the Kansas River when he received orders from Lieutenant Colonel Phillip St. George Cooke. Captain Wood was dispatched to Ozawkie and Hickory Point to accompany a deputy marshal in the service of several writs. The captain was to "aid in the arrest of certain criminals and protect the settlements of peaceable citizens north of the Kansas from robbery and outrage."[87]

With so many people committing outrages on every side, it is difficult to ascertain who and how many "peaceable citizens" actually resided in the territory, but nonetheless, they were to be protected. It took the captain hours to get his command across the Kansas River because of the limited ferry capacity. He again was delayed crossing the Grasshopper (or Delaware) River, but he sent out messengers who reported that night that a man by the name of Harvey commanded a force of 350 men and artillery. Free state settlers had been attacked by the forces. According to Captain Wood, Harvey was designated a colonel "among the organized disturbers of the peace of the Territory."[88]

A few hours after crossing the Grasshopper, Captain Wood ran into a party of twenty-five armed men; they admitted that they were part of Harvey's command and had been engaged in the battle at Hickory Point.

"The deputy marshal arrested them in the name of the United States," wrote Captain Wood,[89] who captured 101 prisoners, forty-seven of Sharp's carbines, thirty-eight muskets, six hunting knives, two shotguns, twenty revolvers, fourteen Bowie knives, four swords, one cannon, a "large amount of ammunition for all" and twenty-seven horses, plus harness horses. This was very impressive but also problematic, especially the prisoners. Lieutenant Colonel Cooke immediately requested that Governor Geary take the prisoners into "his keeping," as their presence "embarrasses the troops and diminishes their efficiency." The officer also said that he could offer the marshal and sheriff "some aid" in moving the prisoners if they were not taken farther than Lecompton.[90]

There was one death and several injuries from the encounter at Hickory Point. It is incredible to think that in two months' time, Governor Geary and General Smith would each declare that the Kansas Territory was at peace, believing that any insurrections had been quelled and that settlers were tired of fighting and ready to *settle*. The eternally optimistic Cyrus K. Holliday, visiting in Pennsylvania, soon wrote to his friend, Franklin Crane, who was yet in Topeka. His letter was full of plans for the future of his adopted home, plans to purchase a "lithograph" for reproducing maps and plans for the wave of immigration sure to happen in the spring. It also stressed the very important relationship between the growing territory and the nation's capital, as well as the importance of selecting a strong representative:

> *I think that you have abandoned the idea of coming East this Winter. I hope you have: for I really do not see how they can well do without you at Topeka. You have such a "run" of all the transactions of the Association*

that it seems to me that no one would be able to supply your place. Still at the same time there are some things that ought to be attended to in the East and which only you can correctly attend. I have reference chiefly to the procuring of a Lithograph for Topeka, as you mentioned in your letter before the last. It will be necessary for Topeka to exert every energy to maintain her present high reputation during the immense emigration that will take place the coming Spring…

Your writing to Senator Brodhead concerning the Bridge appropriation was a most excellent thought—If I only had the money to go on and lobby at Washington for a couple of months I have no doubt but that I could both procure an appropriation for the Topeka Bridge; but, in the general system of spoliation now going on at the Capital, could also procure appropriations of Lands for a RailRoad from Leavenworth to Topeka— and from the mouth of the Kansas River to Ft. Riley by way of Topeka—I have thought of this matter much but am too confounded poor to put it in execution—We must see to this next session of Congress, if that is not too late, and for this purpose must see that a proper man is returned the next time to Congress—a man who can do something for us…your Topeka Bridge—I like the idea much—Write soon—Love to Thornton, Paul &c. &c. I & my family will certainly come by the "first Boat."

Yours very truly
C.K. Holliday

Chapter 11

Another Enemy

Isaac Cody struggled with his health and threats from proslavery neighbors but continued his efforts to populate the Kansas Territory with antislavery followers. In the autumn of 1856, he went to Cleveland, Ohio, to visit one of his brothers and perhaps get some much-needed rest, but he was also recruiting settlers. In December, he attended a banquet in Chicago and met Abraham Lincoln, a cousin to Cody's friend in the territory, Mark Delahay. He delivered a letter from Delahay to the lawyer from Illinois.

Returning to the Kansas Territory in January, Isaac—and those he had induced to make Kansas their homes—waited for the spring weather. When April arrived, it brought an outbreak of measles and scarlet fever among the settlers. Julia Cody Goodman said that her father helped bury a little girl in the pouring rain and got a chill. He died four days later.

"These two children [Julia and Bill, also referred to as Willie] had suffered enough animosity from neighbors and former friends to demoralize any but the strong," commented historian John S. Gray, "having lost their father and breadwinner, they were suddenly left with a mother, resolute but ailing, and four younger siblings to care for. To their everlasting credit, they rose nobly to the challenge."[91]

Twelve-year-old Bill took over the farming, and his older sister worked at the household chores. That summer, he took a job hauling hay to Fort Leavenworth for a neighbor, and later that year he worked for Majors and Russell as a messenger between its office and Fort Leavenworth. Though he could not know it then, the army was already making decisions that would change the course of his life.

When General Persifor F. Smith, commanding the Department of the West, declared the territory at peace, he added, "Being no longer occupied with the affairs in this Territory which have caused so much uneasiness, undivided attention can be paid to punishing the Cheyenne Indians."[92]

In October 1856, Secretary of War Jefferson Davis wrote that "the demand for troops arising from the disturbed condition of the Territory of Kansas, deprived the department the power to execute its plans in relation to the Cheyenne Indians."[93]

While the energies of most of the Western Command and public officials had been taken up with the political strife of Bleeding Kansas, Captain H.W. Wharton was dealing with a different situation. On September 8, 1856, he reported to the War Department:

> *I would likewise state that the Cheyenne Indians have been committing a series of depredations for some months past…*
>
> *A discharged soldier from Fort Laramie came in last evening and reports that he left there in company with some Mormons who were returning to the States; that on the 6th instant, he was out hunting buffalo a short distance from his camp, and on returning to it, he found the Indians had killed two men, one woman and a child, and had carried off one woman; they also drove off all their animals and set fire to the wagon. This man is the only one of the party that escaped. A small party is also reported to have been murdered on the "Little Blue." Depredations have for years been frequent in this last named vicinity; and as it is the grand rendezvous for several tribes, a military post is much needed there.[94]*

The first months of 1857 saw a troop drawdown in the eastern half of the territory, with some shift to the western half and the Nebraska border. Colonel Edwin Sumner led the punitive expedition against the Cheyennes.

Somewhere along the Solomon River, near present-day Morland, Kansas, the United States cavalry rounded a bluff and saw something moving in the distant trees that at first appeared to be buffalo. Through their field glasses, the officers could see that they were actually Indians, "and a swarm of them…mounting and moving this way." The Cheyennes had been waiting several hours and had been grazing their horses. The cavalry mounts, on the other hand, were "quite jaded." The Cheyennes greatly outnumbered the cavalry, and as they rode forward, they were screaming as if "all the fiends from Heaven that fell Had pealed the battle-cry of Hell."[95]

"Things happen pretty lively and thought flies like lightning at such a time," recalled Private Robert Morris Peck. "I remember to have thought, as I made a mental estimate of our chances, while we got into line, 'Of course we'll have to whip them, for it's a groundhog case; but I wish the infantry and battery were here, for I'm afraid "Old Bull" has bit off more than he can chew.' If the colonel thought anything of the kind there was no sign of it, for he never hesitated, but went right ahead as though the prospect just suited him. The men used to say they believed he would fight a buzz saw."[96]

There were Pawnee and Delaware Indians with the cavalry acting as interpreters, or just warriors who thrilled at the power of U.S. forces in a fight with their old enemies. As the Cheyennes came within range, a Delaware chief rode out between the foes, halted his horse and raised his rifle to fire a shot at the Cheyennes. The enemy heartily returned fire as the Delawares turned and rejoined his ranks.

Colonel Sumner bellowed, "Bear witness…An Indian fired the first shot!" It was supposed that the colonel had orders not to fire first, and the fact that the Indian who started the battle was in *his* command would not be included in his report.

Lieutenant J.E.B. Stuart described what happened as the two forces collided:

> [W]e overtook about 500 Cheyennes drawn up in order of battle and marching boldly and steadily towards us. It was my intention & I believe that of most company commanders to give a carbine volley & then charge with drawn pistols…But much to my surprise the Col. ordered draw sabre charge when the Indians were within gun shot. We set up a terrific yell which Scattered the Cheyennes in a disorderly flight & we therefore kept up the charge in pursuit.[97]

The Cheyennes had prepared themselves for guns. Their medicine man, perhaps it was White Bull, told them to bathe in a certain pool that it would either prevent the guns from firing or make them impervious to the bullets.

Another Enemy

Private Peck continued:

> *He* [Sumner] *seemed to have determined to offset the disparity of numbers by a bold dash that would create a panic in the enemy's ranks, and roared out, "Sling—carbines!" then immediately, "Draw—sabers!" and we knew the old man was going to try a saber charge on them.*
>
> *I noticed with some surprise that when the command "Draw—saber" was given (which I then thought was a serious mistake in the colonel) and our three hundred bright blades flashed out of their scabbards, the Cheyennes, who were coming on at a lope, checked up. The sight of so much cold steel seemed to cool their ardor. The party that had started to cross the river after passing our right also hesitated, and Captain Beall, with his company deployed to the left, easily turned back those that were turning our left flank. I then said to myself, "I guess 'Old Bull' knows what he's doing after all."*[98]

Two privates and an estimated thirty Cheyennes were killed, though the small encounters were strung out over seven miles and it was difficult to count. One Cheyenne surrendered—an anomaly, thought the soldiers. The Delawares performed admirably, noted Peck, but the Pawnees swept in after the battle, scalping the dead and taking their ponies. Then the Pawnees went to Sumner and proposed a trade: the sixty ponies they had just confiscated, plus the pay they were to receive back at Fort Stephen Kearney, in exchange for the Cheyenne prisoner. They greatly desired perform a scalp dance and then torture the man to death. Colonel Sumner was so disgusted that he not only turned them down but also dismissed them on the spot. The next morning, the disgruntled Indians began the walk back to their village near Fort Kearney, Nebraska Territory.[99]

Among the twelve wounded soldiers was Lieutenant Stuart. He had been shot in the shoulder by an "unhorsed Cheyenne whose life Stuart was trying to save," recalled Peck. "It is possible that the Indian misunderstood his intentions."[100]

When the troops moved out, the wounded and a half company of men to guard them were left behind to recuperate. Fearing that the Cheyennes might return, an earthen fort was hastily constructed. "We turned to and threw up a sod-and-dirt wall about five feet high," wrote Private Peck, "enclosing a square plot of probably about fifty feet each way—large enough to contain the little garrison and their animals."[101]

Lieutenant Stuart dubbed the earthworks "Fort Floyd," and while lying there, shaded by a piece of canvas, he would go over the battle again and again in his mind. Lieutenant Stuart took out a pencil and sketched a device that would hold a saber to the belt and allow it to be removed more quickly. He may have envisioned earning a lot of money from this little invention, but likely he had no idea that it would soon put him in the middle of one of the most historic events of the Civil War.

Colonel Sumner and his men burned the hastily deserted Cheyenne village, and some of his cavalry then headed southwest to Bent's Fort (which was in the Kansas Territory then but is now in Colorado), where the famished soldiers restocked their rations. At Big Bend, the mail was intercepted on the Santa Fe route bearing orders for Sumner to report back to Fort Leavenworth but also for his command to join that of Brevet Brigadier General Albert Sidney Johnston, en route to Utah to put down the Brigham Young rebellion. Sumner informed his men that he would let the War Department know that they were worn out and would have to go no farther than Fort Kearney. He was good to his word, and when they arrived in Nebraska, they found that other soldiers had been sent to take care of the Mormons.

As for the men left behind, Lieutenant Stuart, though his arm was disabled by his wound, was "still worth a half-dozen ordinary men," recalled Peck, "for Jeb was always prolific of expedients for working his way out of difficult or embarrassing situations." The young captain who had been left in charge had not ample means to transport wounded men. Old lodge poles were found next to the river, and Stuart soon improvised. Stretchers were made of the poles "by fastening a piece of stout canvas—pack-covers—across the center of each two poles, then hitching a pack-mule—one before and one behind—between the ends of the poles, which were lashed to the pack-saddles—the front mule's tail to the wounded man and the rear one's head—with a man to walk alongside and lead each mule carefully, a very comfortable litter was formed."[102]

The soldiers then moved eastward and were back in time for peacekeeping during the Kansas Territorial elections. After patrolling the northeast, the cavalry was sent south to polling places in Humboldt and Fort Scott. Likewise they were assigned the task of tracking down the "ubiquitous abolitionist" James Montgomery, "who was said to be raising hades with the 'peaceable and law-abiding citizens of Missouri.'"[103]

The Lecompton Constitution allowing slavery was approved, and the Kansas Territory applied to Congress for statehood.

Chapter 12
Peculiar Minds

The man John Brown had described as peculiar was in his element considering his companions. A stranger person than John Montgomery would be difficult to find, unless, of course, one were describing James H. Lane, whose photographs almost appear in motion, with his long hair waving wildly. Or perhaps Charles Leonhardt, the fanatic Prussian? It seemed that the Kansas Territory was full of peculiar people. Of this group, Montgomery may have actually been the closest to normal. And comparing a photo of Montgomery to the group above, he appears positively *dull*.

Not prone to the rousing speechmaking of Lane, Montgomery did instill confidence and inspired men to follow him. Historian Brian Dirck noted that Montgomery's leadership talents were not easy to identify, but like Brown and others in Bleeding Kansas, he was given to "righteous violence," that belief that his actions no matter how extreme were justified by the cause. He was a man who marched to his own drummer, to be sure, but perhaps more quietly than his colleagues. He possessed nerve and personal courage; he was not nearly as excitable as, say, Brown or Lane—except for an incident with a ballot box. The territory was voting on whether or not to ratify the Lecompton Constitution, which, of course, allowed slavery to be extended into Kansas. Having some pretty reliable information that the ballot box had been stuffed by proslavery voters in Linn County, he strode though the crowd and physically smashed the box, exclaiming that he was defending the rights of free men.[104]

Even with all the violence and horror that had been perpetrated during the years of Bleeding Kansas, interfering with an election in this manner was frowned upon. Montgomery was indicted but never tried for the incident. Though John Brown was more "conspicuous," both he and Montgomery were recognized as free state leaders in the southeastern portion of the territory. The term "Jayhawking" is said to have begun with Montgomery. He was one of the reasons the incidents of Bleeding Kansas shifted from the northeastern portion of the territory to the southeastern.

Montgomery formed a "self-protective company" to defend his neighborhood from the incursions of Missourians. Having lost his own home to raids, Montgomery had more than an idealistic commitment to a cause; he believed that inflicting a loss for a loss would stop the incursions into Kansas. His "company" assumed an offensive position as well. Conducting frequent raids into Missouri, he is said to have had a rule that every man riding with him should be riding a horse or mule stolen from proslavers. Montgomery, with a well-armed force backing him up, ordered the most "rabid" proslavery settlers from the area.[105] But it was his raid in Kansas itself that would ensure his place in the history books.

Audie Murphy
Tony Curtis
BRIAN DONLEVY
MARGUERITE CHAPMAN
SCOTT BRADY
RICHARD LONG

Kansas Raiders

Produced by: Ted Richmond
Screenplay by:
Robert L. Richards
Released: 1951
Running Time: 80 min.
Available in Color

The West's most desperate outlaws...
blazed their names in history!

Kansas Raiders was another film based on the events of the Kansas/Missouri Border War, and it contains almost no historical accuracy except for the names. Brian Donlevy played Quantrill, and war hero Audie Murphy portrayed Jesse James. In fact, Jesse James did not ride with Quantrill, though his brother, Frank, did and was present at the Lawrence Massacre. Later, Jesse rode with Bill Anderson. *Universal Television.*

Fort Scott had been one of those stations in the chain of forts along the "Permanent Indian Frontier," and it was established by 1842, so it made contributions during the Mexican-American War as well. It, like Fort Leavenworth, never had a palisade or wall of any kind. The army abandoned Fort Scott in 1853, and in 1855 the buildings were sold at auction, which created some tense situations when pro- and antislavery folks purchased structures side by side. The community of Fort Scott evolved into one with proslavery leanings, while the surrounding community was mostly populated by free state advocates. The southeastern corner of the territory had no river dividing it from Missouri like the northeast, so raids back and forth were much easier.

As spring came to the territory, raids also became more frequent. Just as the Pottawatomie Massacre had sent shockwaves through eastern Kansas in 1856, the Marais des Cygnes Massacre in May 1858 left the populace in terror. What is astounding in examining the details of the Marais des Cygnes Massacre is that it did not occur in secret but rather unfolded in front of an entire community, with residents standing back until it was too late for anyone to intervene.

Historian Harvey Hougen described what began as a lovely day. Patrick Ross, a Bourbon County farmer, passed through Trading Post at about 8:00 a.m. He was headed to work a claim that Border Ruffians had forced him to vacate weeks before. Just outside the village, he encountered Captain Charles Hamilton leading a band of armed horsemen. He was immediately taken prisoner. Captain Hamilton systematically went through the community, taking men, releasing men, ransacking homes and terrorizing families. At another home, William Stilwell had left early to reach Kansas City and pick up some machinery. With rumors of raids, his wife was concerned for his safety and asked him not to go. It wasn't long before he, too, was a captive, and the line of prisoners was getting longer.[106]

Judge L.D. Bailey, who had moved to the territory in 1857 from New Hampshire, recalled that these Missourians had no motive other than revenge. As the years of warfare on the Kansas/Missouri border indicate, however, revenge can be a very effective motivator. Judge Bailey recalled that about three miles from Trading Post, the captives were lined up in a ravine near Dry Creek. Hougen continued:

> As the ravine narrowed, the captives marched at the bottom in single file, finally halting beneath a wide rock shelf. The Ruffians remained on

horseback, occupying both slopes of the ravine, while the eleven prisoners stood in line, facing eastward. William Hairgrove, the white-haired patriarch, insolently stared upward at this antagonists. "Gentlemen," he growled, "if you are going to shoot us take good aim."

"Make ready!" Hamilton commanded. "Take aim!" Then a moment's hesitation. "The men don't obey the order, Captain," shouted Dr. George Hamilton. The irrepressible Old Man Hairgrove appeared to be more angry than fearful. "They are a good deal like as we are—we don't want to kill innocent persons," he sneered from the bottom of the ravine. Ignoring the remark, Hamilton issued the commands a second time, to no effect.[107]

Captive William Stillwell gave the Masonic sign for distress, raising his arms over his head. At this, one of the horsemen wheeled to ride away, to the rage of Captain Hamilton. The man refused to have anything to do with "such a God damned piece of business as this."[108]

Hamilton ordered the men to fire once more, and he fired the first round himself. Five were killed instantly; one of the injured staggered and begged for mercy, only to be shot in the head. Others were finished off; all were left for dead. Austin Hall was drenched in the blood of his comrades but was uninjured.[109]

Judge Bailey was acquainted with the survivors of the massacre and described the fate of the only Missourian who took part and was ever brought to justice. During the course of the Civil War, William Hairgrove was in Parkville, Missouri, and recognized one of the assailants, William Griffith. He was arrested and immediately demanded that he be shot. Judge Bailey recalled:

They explained to him that he was to be taken back to Linn county and should have a fair trial before the court, but he declared there was no use in going to so much bother; that, they had better take him out and shoot him and be done with it. He was overruled in that, however, and was taken to Linn county, indicted for murder and arraigned for trial before Judge Solon O. Thacher, from whom I had the narrative soon after it occurred. He pled guilty and refused to employ counsel, and when Judge Thacher refused to receive his plea of guilty, ordered a plea of "not guilty" be entered for him and assigned able counsel to defend him. He steadily persisted in declaring himself guilty and ready to suffer the penalty. The witnesses were produced and swore to the facts and the jury of course found him guilty.

The judge then asked the usual question—if he had anything to say before the sentence of death should be passed, when, instead of pleading for mercy, he surprised the judge by asking to be taken right out and hung at once.

The judge told him kindly that he wished to give him time to prepare for death and would set the day of execution two months ahead. But he persisted in asking to be hung at once, saying repeatedly that "he hadn't any clean clothes and wanted it over with." He was perfectly cool—reiterated the talk about not "having clean clothes"—was finally given a month for preparation, much against his wish and was duly hung on the day appointed, seemingly glad when the time came round so that he could get the ugly job off his mind and be done with it.[110]

Ironically, Griffith was well treated while awaiting execution in the Mound City jail, where one minister even baptized the tearful prisoner. For several days, Griffith's wife and small children were hosted by a prominent family, the town thus allowing her to spend precious time with her condemned husband. On the appointed day, soldiers escorted Griffith to a copse of trees where the scaffold had been erected. Anvils were to be used as weights. When asked if he had any last words, he thanked the townspeople for their kindnesses. They had also taken up a collection to pay for his coffin and expenses, giving his widow the balance.[111]

By the end of May, communities in Missouri braced for the reprisal sure to come for the Marais des Cygnes massacre. Some towns formed militias. The insults and attacks by Kansas guerrillas "have forced us to stand guard day and night, to go armed about our daily avocations," wrote Missourians petitioning their government for protection.[112] Indeed, the very evening of the Marais des Cygnes Massacre, James Montgomery returned home from business and led nearly two hundred men into Missouri on a fruitless search for the murderers.

Once again, John Greenleaf Whittier immortalized the victims in a poem. "Le Marais des Cygne" was yet another anthem for the free state cause. As the victims entered the realm of martyrdom, abolitionists' fires were fueled.

In another one of the many attempts by territorial governors to just stop the violence and not bother to sort out the convoluted question of who started it, Governor James Denver issued an amnesty for partisans of both sides if they ceased hostilities. Perhaps the cash-strapped territorial government was out of

Charles Leonhardt, a Prussian who moved to Kansas, was an outspoken abolitionist and was associated with James Montgomery.

money for printing writs and warrants. The amnesty eased tensions, but the lull in violence was an uneasy one. As historian Jeremy Neely summed up the situation, "Settlers on each side were eager to see justice served and thus were reluctant to let the crimes of the past go unpunished."[113]

The truce proved a thin veneer over seething hatred. In October, James Montgomery's home was fired upon. Inside were John Kagi, associate of John Brown, and others. Montgomery wasn't hit but he wasn't happy. The peace was over. Then Benjamin Rice and John Hudlow, two of Montgomery's men, were arrested. This was viewed as a breach of faith since these actions should have been covered by the amnesty. Gathering dozens of men from Linn, Bourbon and Osage Counties, including Charles Leonhardt, Montgomery prepared to attack the community of Fort Scott. Sam Wood came with men from Lawrence. Preston B. Plumb came from Emporia.[114]

The dawn raid resulted in some random pilfering and the successful rescue of the prisoners. Killed in the process was John Little, shopkeeper and former marshal. In defending the town, Little fired at the raiders and struck one in the hand. A shot was then fired that hit Little in the forehead, killing him instantly.[115] Little was a popular man. His murder did not sit well, and more guerrilla violence followed. As Neely said, the politics of the violence was beginning to recede, and it increasingly took the form of simple banditry and harassment against innocent families.

During this time, John Brown reappeared in Kansas. Whether he wrought the violence or sprang from it, they seemed always to come together.

Chapter 13

Battle of the Spurs

In January 1859, the Sheridan family, who lived just outside Topeka, were on the lookout for John Brown. He was on the way, and he was bringing slaves from Missouri. Historian L.L. Kiene wrote of Brown:

> *The aged emancipator had reached the period of life when his very name was a terror to the slave-owners and also to the local officers under the United States or the provisional government of Kansas. The president of the United States had set a price upon the head of Brown, and this had been supplemented by rewards by the governors of Missouri and Kansas. To the slavery sympathizers he was the red-handed murderer of innocent men who opposed him, but to the Sheridans and other anti-slavery advocates he was a benign, fatherly individual, whose voice was seldom raised except in denunciation of human slavery.*[116]

Having been in the East making speeches, gaining support and mostly raising money, Brown had returned to the battlefield. On December 20, 1858, he divided his men into two forces, one to be led by himself and the other by John Kagi, who was using the alias of Stevens. They raided farms in western Missouri, taking eleven slaves and killing a slaveholder. Charles Leonhardt appeared confidant that he had the basic facts in the incident:

> *About John Brown going into Missouri after these slaves. This is the fact in the case: a negro slave who had permission by his master to go into fort*

scott for the purpose of selling brooms which he made, found enough news to tell him if could possibly see Capt. John brown & tell him his troubles he would help him to freedom. This slave either found the Captains camp or he must have met with Kagi. He told Kagi that he and his wife and children were to be sold next Tuesday and begged him on his journey north. Kagi replied that Capt Brown was absent but that he would ____ the captain & __ _____ he could depend _____ their help. Kagi instructed that this slave get his family & friends ready the evening before the sale they would certainly come & help him. [117]

This question of if or how slaves knew they would be liberated is often asked. In this case, Kagi had promised that the rescuers would be there the night before the sale; according to Leonhardt's account, when John Brown heard of their plight, he said that they should step it up a day—the raid would be more difficult the night before the sale. Thus, the slaves were taken by surprise and unprepared when the raiders arrived. Leonhardt wanted to stress, too, that it was Kagi and not Brown who deserved the credit for stealing the slaves. [118]

Raids into Missouri were increasing in number and destructiveness, and Brown and Kagi were not the only abolitionists helping fugitive slaves. Later in January, John Doy, his son, Charles, and another man from Lawrence were escorting thirteen slaves when a proslavery posse from Lawrence intercepted them and took them to Weston, Missouri. Doy was tried in St. Joseph and sentenced to five years in the Missouri penitentiary. Before he was transported, a group of his friends from Lawrence led by James Abbott, the same man who had been involved in the rescue of Jacob Branson, broke into the jail and threatened to kill the jailer if Doy were not released. [119]

As one might imagine, no matter how noble the intent may have been, the act of breaking a convicted felon out of jail was controversial. Abbott and his men were either heroes or outlaws, with no middle ground.

For the slaves Brown and Kagi had liberated, the road to freedom was slow. It was a month after the raid before they had reached Lawrence, and then they traveled to Topeka, where Brown stayed with his old friend John Ritchie. The slaves, now numbering twelve since a baby had been born along the escape route, were secreted here and there around Topeka with Ritchie's friends, the "Topeka Boys."

The Topeka Boys comprised a network of early settlers who fought against the Border Ruffians and collaborated to assist fugitive slaves to freedom, according to historian William O. Wagnon. As a network, they functioned much as the popular myth of the Underground Railroad was portrayed.

"Considerable attention has been given to the notion that the Underground Railroad was more legend than fact," wrote Wagnon. Historians have demonstrated that relatively few slaves escape through the assistance of antislavery activists. Most slaves who escaped did so as individuals. Once again, Kansas was a different story. Wagnon continued:

> *In the Kansas Territory free black communities had not had time to develop, but abolitionist-minded white communities did. These communities were created with the avowed purpose of reversing the initial control of the territory by proslavery activists in 1855 and 1856. Topeka was just such a community. The "Topeka Boys," who had earlier formed a militia to defend free-state individuals and communities reconfigured their activities by 1857 into helping slaves elude their pursuers, once their community was secure. For Topeka abolitionists and their passengers, the Underground Railroad was a reality.*[120]

The home of John and Mary Jane Ritchie, on the edge of town in Topeka's early years and now virtually the heart of it, was an important link in the line of safe houses that made up this network in the Kansas Territory. John Ritchie claimed that he and his wife had helped liberate $100,000 worth of human chattel. It was a dangerous business, as the arrest of Doy demonstrated. Ritchie was among those free staters arrested and imprisoned for a time in Lecompton in 1856. He escaped and returned to his home state of Indiana until it was safe to return to the Kansas Territory. During his absence, Mary Jane continued to aid escaping slaves. It was not unusual for a posse of armed horsemen to surround the house in search of fugitives at any hour of the day.[121]

The Ritchies developed a close relationship with Brown, though their goals were not exactly the same. While Brown wanted to abolish slavery, he really had no vision beyond that. Ritchie did. He wanted to build a community based on principles of equality. He wanted to not only end slavery but also create opportunities for education and employment. In these sentiments, he had few peers. Brown met with Ritchie and other members of the Topeka Boys in 1859 and may have discussed his coming raid on Harpers Ferry. If he did, the Topekans declined to participate. They understood their mission differently. There had to

John Ritchie moved from Indiana to Kansas in 1855 and was active in the free state community as an operator on the Underground Railroad and in helping freed blacks find homes and jobs. He was a friend and supporter of John Brown and was one of the "Topeka Boys," a group of businessmen dedication to the abolition of slavery. *Shawnee County Historical Society.*

be a future for blacks once freed. They were building that community. And again it was that community that would come to the aid of Brown as he was leaving Kansas one final time.

When Brown and his group had arrived, there was great care in keeping his presence secret. He remained inside during the day, while Ritchie and others went about town collecting items of clothing for the fugitives. As night fell, the entourage crossed the Kansas River. Jacob Willits escorted them, and even though the weather had been mild for January, the night wind was chilling. He noticed Brown shivering. A historian recorded:

> *The wind blew along the water from the north, rippling the surface and causing the aged emancipator to shiver. Willits noticed this and said: "I don't believe that you have enough clothes for the weather." "Do not bother about me. There are others not so well supplied."*
>
> *Willits then took hold of Brown's trousers and found that he wore no underclothing, and after they had crossed the river he induced Brown to take those he wore, the exchange being made by the roadside.*[122]

With muddy conditions, the travel northward was slow, but once the group had passed through the town of Holton without incident, they thought that there was no longer a need to travel at night. The next day, they reached a stop on the Underground Railroad, six miles northwest of Holton, the home of Albert Fuller. They determined to stay the night, as the horses were exhausted. One of Brown's men, Aaron Stevens, went to a nearby stream for water and came upon two mounted deputy marshals.

One marshal inquired if Stevens had seen any slaves around, and to the officer's surprise, Stevens replied that yes, there were slaves in that cabin. One marshal went to the cabin with Stevens, while the other tended horses. Upon entering, the youthful marshal found himself looking down the barrels of two revolvers. He was taken prisoner, and it was discovered that he was one of a posse led by John P. Wood, a deputy U.S. marshal from Lecompton. The fugitives were frantic. Had they come through all these trials, to be so close to freedom, only to be caught now?

The posse was entrenched a little ways from the cabin. Brown managed to sneak a messenger out that night with instructions to get word of the situation to John Ritchie.

Ritchie was already in his pew at the Congregationalist Church when his friend John Armstrong came in and whispered to him. As Ritchie hurried out, Reverend Lewis Bodwell excused himself to investigate, and upon hearing of the situation, he dismissed the service. Many of the congregation members, with as much secrecy as possible, prepared for a number of their men to ride to Brown's aid.

They arrived as Brown's party was preparing to continue its journey, despite the posse watching their every move from the rifle pits that they had hastily constructed. It appeared to be suicidal to go on. Mother Nature appeared to be on the side of the posse, as the rain had swelled Straight Creek to dangerous levels. Historian L.L. Kliene reported the exchange:

> *"What do you propose to do, captain?" asked one of the body-guard.*
>
> *"Cross the creek and move north," he responded, and his lips closed in that familiar, firm expression which left no doubt as to his purpose.*
>
> *"But, captain, the water is high and the Fuller crossing is very bad. I doubt if we can get through. There is a much better ford five miles up the creek," said one of the men who joined the rescuers at Holton.*

The old man faced the guard, and his eyes flashed. "I have set out on the Jim Lane road," he said, "and I intend to travel it straight through, and there is no use to talk of turning aside. Those who are afraid may go back, but I will cross at the Fuller crossing. The Lord has marked out a path for me and I intend to follow it. We are ready to move."[123]

His followers may have thought him crazy, and their faith may have not matched his, but they fell in and crossed with him, even as the guns of their enemy were trained on them. Kliene continued:

Did the men who were waiting know that with a single volley they could wipe John Brown and his guard from the face of the earth? They certainly did, but what force was it that kept their fingers from their triggers? Perhaps the moral courage of the old man had paralyzed their arms.

John Brown appeared utterly oblivious of the presence of Wood and his forces. He looked straight ahead as if the deputy marshal and his men had been ants…On toward the ford went the little company of Kansans. They did not fire a shot and not a gun was raised.[124]

The posse members ran for their horses to pursue, but instead their ranks became a panic. As the horses twisted and turned in the mad rush, one or two of the men wound up grabbing the tail of his horse and was dragged across the prairie. (This gave the encounter its name, "Battle of the Spurs.") The Topekans gave chase and captured four men who had thrown down their arms in the rifle pits. In the meantime, the wagon had become mired in the creek, and it was hours before it was pried loose. Ritchie and his friends accompanied Brown's group to Seneca and then turned and came home. Brown continued to Iowa, delivering each and every one of the fugitives to freedom.

Chapter 14

Treason

In October 1859, Lieutenant J.E.B. Stuart was on leave from his service in the frontier army in Kansas Territory. He had visited family in Patrick County, Virginia, and then had gone to Richmond to attend a convention of Episcopal laymen. Though fun-loving and by outward appearances somewhat of a partygoer, Stuart was devout and a confirmed nondrinker. He had set the cornerstone of the Episcopal church in Junction City, Kansas Territory, and he and his wife were active in the congregation.

While in Richmond, Lieutenant Stuart was called to Washington for a meeting at the War Department. Officials were interested in the device the officer had developed for attaching a saber to a belt. He was in a waiting room when news arrived that there was trouble in Harpers Ferry, Virginia. The lieutenant was asked to deliver the news to Colonel Robert E. Lee, who was also home on leave. Lee had been Stuart's superintendent at West Point years before. Stuart asked to accompany Lee to the site of the insurrection. There were no army troops available, so the War Department sent ninety marines under the command of Lieutenant Israel Green. Meanwhile, Lieutenant Stuart, Colonel Lee and Secretary of War John B. Floyd were conferring with President James Buchanan at the White House. The chief executive signed a proclamation of martial law, gave Lee command of all forces at Harpers Ferry and appointed Stuart as his aide. They arrived soon after the marines.

Harpers Ferry is picturesquely located on the confluence of the Potomac and Shenandoah Rivers, west of Washington, D.C. There was a federal arsenal located in the village, a stop on the Baltimore and Ohio Railroad.

This movie still from *Santa Fe Trail* depicts one of the few historically accurate moments in the film. It portrays John Brown (Raymond Massey) opening the door of the engine house at Harpers Ferry, Virginia. Standing just outside with terms of surrender is Lieutenant J.E.B. Stuart (Errol Flynn). *Author's collection, Warner Bros.*

By the time the officers and marines arrived, local militia had been battling a small group of raiders that was now holed up in the fire engine house. There had apparently been an attempt to take over the arsenal. A dozen men on both sides were dead, including the town's mayor. The apparent leader of the group had identified himself as "Smith," though he had identified himself as "Osawatomie Brown of Kansas" to some of his prisoners. His true identity was not established until Lieutenant Stuart arrived.

Colonel Lee wrote out the terms of surrender that would be presented to the outlaws. If they were not accepted, their position would be immediately attacked by the marines. Lieutenant Stuart, under a flag of truce, walked to the door and announced his presence. Through the closed door, he read, "Colonel Lee, United States Army, commanding the troops sent by the President of the United States to suppress the insurrection at this place, demands the surrender of the persons in the Armory buildings."

Then the leader came to the door, and Lieutenant Stuart saw a familiar face:

> *He opened the door about four inches and placed his body against the crack, with a cocked carbine in his hands: hence his remark after his capture that he could have wiped me out like a mosquito…When Smith first came to the door I recognized old Osawatomie Brown who had given us so much trouble in Kansas.*
>
> *Old Brown was talkative…*
>
> *"Well, Lieutenant, I see we can't agree. You have the numbers on me, but you know we soldiers aren't afraid of death. I would as leave die by the bullet as on the gallows."*
>
> *"Is that your final answer, Captain?"*
>
> *"Yes," Brown said.*
>
> *Stuart stepped aside and waved his hat.*[125]

In this still from the movie *Santa Fe Trail*, John Brown (Raymond Massey) and his men are shown following the Battle of Black Jack. In a "nearly historically correct" portrayal, Brown does meet Lieutenant J.E.B. Stuart face to face, a chance meeting that would serve Stuart well three years later at Harpers Ferry, Virginia. *Author's collection, Warner Bros.*

The marines stormed the engine house, and the entire fight lasted only minutes. Brown was struck unconscious by a sword and carried to a nearby office. As his wounds were treated and he regained consciousness, Brown was questioned as to his motives and supporters. He had expected help, he said, from both whites and blacks. He was disappointed that it had not come. He had hoped that a full-scale slave rebellion would begin with his small band of his sons and followers.

When news of the raid reached Kansas, many of the territory's leaders were virtually tripping over themselves to deny knowledge, support or association with Brown. One of his contemporaries said, "I was by no means an admirer of him while he was in Kansas, considering him altogether too rash."[126]

Charles Robinson appeared before a Congressional committee investigating the raid. "Robinson in his testimony," wrote historian Albert Castel, "sought to clear the Kansas Free State Party of any complicity in the raid by stating that Brown, John Kagi, Josiah Hinton, John Redpath, William Phillips, and others of the Kansas radical faction were never true members of that party and that the troubles in southern Kansas were caused by Lane's military expedition through that region in 1857."[127]

Kansans could hardly be blamed for denying him; treason and conspiracy were not small matters. Brown was charged with treason against the Commonwealth of Virginia and put on trial in Charlestown. That he would be found guilty was a foregone conclusion, as was his death sentence. Not all Kansans were

James Redpath was an ardent follower of John Brown and a correspondent for the *New York Tribune*. His articles provide lively insights into the events of the territorial period. *Kansas State Historical Society.*

so anxious to deny him, however, and even made plans instead to rescue him.

In October, an informal but urgent meeting was held in Linn County, Kansas. James Montgomery was a party to the meeting. There, the plan to head to Virginia was conceived. *How* was the obvious question: a lot of men to storm the jail, or a small party to devise some scheme? Some of the Doy rescue party were obvious picks to save Brown from the noose: Joseph Gardner, Silas S. Soule, Joshua A. Pike and S.J. Willis. Benjamin Rice, who had been rescued at Fort Scott, was willing. D.R. Anthony, newspaper publisher and brother of the suffragist, recalled that sometime in November 1859 James Montgomery visited him and told him of the plan. He needed funds and Anthony loaned him $150. The rescue party boarded a train a few miles east of St. Joseph, Missouri, and traveled to Pittsburgh, Pennsylvania, where Silas Soule met the party. When they arrived in Harrisburg, there was a meeting with the Honorable R.J. Hinton of New York.[128] Joshua Pike recalled:

> *From that meeting scouts were sent out into Maryland and Virginia. Soule went to Charlestown and talked with Brown, two armed guards standing over him. After this country had been looked over carefully, the project was given up. Deep snow, cold weather, United States troops, police officers at all corners, etc. The whole matter was given up and all sent home.*[129]

These were challenges, to be sure, but the greatest challenge was Brown himself. He did not wish to be rescued, in part because his jailer had afforded him special privileges if he promised not to escape; and second, he was worth more dead than alive.

Mahala Doyle, one of the widows from the Pottawatomie Massacre, was gratified to know that Brown would hang and wrote to him from her home in Chattanooga, Tennessee. She thought that he might understand her own sorrow now that he, too, had lost two sons. Her younger son, now grown to manhood, would be there to put the noose around Brown's neck if the governor would allow it. She wrote, "You cant say you done it to free our slaves, we had none and never expected to own one."[130]

Also in jail and awaiting execution was Aaron D. Stevens, who had lived in Kansas. His old friend John Ritchie wrote:

You are in my mind constantly, And I am glad to know that you are so much resigned to your present prison, and the sentence of death on the 16th inst. I can see but one way left for me to be of any service to you and that is to direct your mind to the Saviour. Ye must be born again—Lord I give myself away. Be wise. You do not fear man. Fear the Lord. This is the beginning of wisdom. When you read these lines Remember they are intended for your good, after you leave us here below. Hope in God. If you have any requests…Let me in bidding you a last adieu remind you that you will be remembered in the prayers of many who call upon God in sincerity and truth for the salvation of your never dying soul. May God bless you is my desire. Farewell.[131]

Stevens was hanged on March 16, 1860, along with Albert Hazlett. John Henry Kagi, who once had a shootout with Judge Rush Elmore on the steps of the courthouse in Tecumseh, was killed during the raid. Also killed in the raid was Jeremiah Goldsmith Anderson, who was one of James Montgomery's men. Watson and Oliver Brown, sons of Old Osawatomie, were mortally wounded during the raid. Others died, and others were hanged on December 16.

Brown was hanged on December 2, 1859. Abraham Lincoln, visiting in Leavenworth, Kansas Territory, was asked about the affair. He replied: "Old John Brown has just been executed for treason against the state. We cannot object, even though he agreed with us in thinking slavery wrong. That cannot excuse violence, bloodshed, and treason. It could avail him nothing that he might think himself right."[132] Thomas Ewing, Jr., also an attorney who had made his home in Leavenworth, commented that in all the eulogizing over Brown, his victims were forgotten. Had Brown succeeded in forcing a war between free staters and the American government, the world would have stood with the South, and the "North would have been divided, overwhelmed and conquered."[133]

Though he had not announced his candidacy, Lincoln most assuredly was testing the waters to run for president. In Kansas, he delivered the "rough draft" of what would be the Cooper Union Address delivered in Manhattan, New York. The speech was widely reprinted, and many believe that it was a major factor in Lincoln's election the succeeding fall. Lincoln was a guest of his cousin, Mark Delahay, and spoke at half a dozen venues in the northeast of the territory.

As the spring of 1860 bloomed in the Kansas Territory, the promise of a free state of Kansas seemed secure. The greatest crisis facing settlers was the drought, a desperate situation. Historian Rod Beemer cited Lettie Little Pabst of Lyon County: "If 1859 was a bountiful year, 1860 was the opposite. That was the year of the most horrible drought. Nothing was raised. Only starvation lay ahead. More than a year passed and there was no rain in Lyon County."[134]

Beemer added that the widespread drought resulted in dust storms, with the devastation of livestock a common result. The lack of grass also had the effect of pushing buffalo herds from the high plains eastward. That could account for the rare occurrence of a man in Dickinson County having been gored to death by one of the beasts on September 8, 1860.[135]

"Between the ongoing drought and the slowing economy," noted historian Ronald D. Smith, "all that was holding Leavenworth together was the hope that Congress would admit Kansas as a state before the land dried up and blew away."[136]

No doubt many Topekans were concerned with the dry conditions and the impact on settlement and commerce. Having secured the safety of citizens, expanding the territory and the eventual state were critical to providing the bright future they had planned for themselves and for the freed men and women who would settle in the territory. The Pony Express began delivering mail on April 3, 1860, and it marked progress in connecting the western settlements to the rest of the nation.

Progress was everywhere. John Ritchie was involved in many commercial enterprises in his adopted town. Operating a quarry and lime kiln, developing the town and planning for a university—these were the projects bearing on his mind that April when a federal marshal rode up to his home. The *State Record* of Topeka carried the story under the headline "Terrible Homicide": "An exciting tragedy occurred in our usually quiet town, on yesterday evening, which resulted in the death of Deputy U.S. Marshal L. Arms, at the hands of our fellow townsman, John Ritchey [*sic*]."[137]

The paper went on to detail the political strife that had led to the charges and described the terrible conditions under which Ritchie had been imprisoned in Lecompton. From the time of his escape, said the reporter, proslavery men had been after him. The *State Record* reported:

Constitution Hall in Lecompton, Kansas, was the seat of territorial government, as well as the office for filing land claims. The Lecompton Constitution was written in this building; it was submitted to Congress for the approval of Kansas as a slave state. Eventually, the Wyandotte Constitution was ratified and brought Kansas into the Union as a free state. This is a state historic site today, and Lane University nearby serves as the museum and headquarters of the Lecompton Historical Society. *Photo by Michelle Martin.*

[H]e has been singled out as the victim of persecution and annoyance at the hands of Government officials. Several attempts have heretofore been made to re-arrest him upon the original charge of mail robbery, (than which, we who were familiar with him during the whole time at which the crime is charged, know that nothing could be more utterly fictitious) but until the present time no man has been found fool-hardy enough to persist in an attempt at arrest.[138]

The fact that Deputy Marshal Arms was dead would be evidence of just how foolhardy it was to attempt the arrest of Ritchie. According to Giles, Ritchie and his friend Harvey D. Rice were in the yard when Leonard Arms, accompanied by another man, approached him. He took Ritchie aside and told him that he was there to arrest him on the charges that had been made in 1856 and for which Ritchie had been imprisoned in Lecompton.

It was understood that the amnesty issued by Governor Robert Walker in 1857 had applied to those charges, but then, according to historian Fry Giles, rumors began to circulate in 1860 that those who had been indicted would have to appear and essentially pay court costs to have the dismissals entered. Ritchie was of a like mind with many of his contemporaries who believed that this was not amnesty at all, and he had no intentions of appearing on the trumped-up charges. One of the allegations against Ritchie, said Giles, was the "absurd charge of mail robbery."[139]

Many years later, Rice recalled the incident and said that after the private conversation between Ritchie and Arms, Ritchie motioned to his friend to join them. He told Rice that Arms claimed to be a marshal but had no writs or warrants, and he would not consent to go with him. Arms said that he would be back the next day with reinforcements if Ritchie would not go peaceably. Ritchie went into the house and got a revolver. Arms, who had borrowed a pistol from a townsperson, followed Ritchie inside. It was a tense situation but then it seemed defused; it appeared as both the marshal would leave and the tragedy would be averted. But as Arms reached the door to leave, he changed his mind and turned back to Ritchie, telling him that he would have to go. Ritchie shot him, and the marshal fell dead in the doorway. Mrs. Ritchie, frantic upon hearing the gunshot, ran into the house for their three-year-old son, John, who was screaming, and stumbled over the deputy marshal's body.[140]

Ritchie turned himself in and was ably defended by James H. Lane. It was found that the homicide was justifiable. Legally, it would appear that the fact that Arms did not seem to have warrants with him was enough to call into question his official capacity.

The decision was not without controversy. In May, the *Topeka Tribune* carried an article that was reprinted from the *Olathe Herald*. The item referred to the *Lawrence Republican* and *Leavenworth Times*, which had agreed with the decision not to prosecute Ritchie. The reference to the troubles of Ritchie's friend and attorney Jim Lane are also mentioned. The article noted that no matter the politics of anyone involved, resisting arrest and the killing of a U.S. marshal in the line of duty were not to be sanctioned:

> *They* [the facts] *are indisputable and cannot be gainsayed or denied. If the Republican Press of the Territory wishes to espouse the cause of murderers, assassins, highway robbers, and common thieves we have no objections to interpose, as they naturally belong to that class of humanity, but we must say in justice to a few individual members of the Republican party, as a party, endorses the murder, that they can no longer be found in their ranks, defending the fanaticism and depravity of the party...*

The [Topeka State] *Record wishes to make the affair assume a partisan shape and thereby rally the party to the support of Lane, the murderer of Jenkins, for United States Senator from Kansas. Do the people, the "bone and sinew" of Kansas wish to degrade themselves by resorting to such perfidy, and disgraceful conduct? We think not, and feel confident that a large mass of our citizens are prepared to deal out justice to John Ritchey, or any other offender of the laws, without the fear of being assassinated, or politically damned by those would leaders and fanatics.*[141]

Rice recalled that there were rumors that Ritchie would be killed and that he had gone into hiding. Rice helped his friend find a secure place to remain out of sight due to the angry threats. Still, when Ritchie returned home after a few weeks, he did so in the company of several "protectors," including Rice.[142]

Later that year, the news turned from the Ritchie/Arms affair to the national election. Republican Abraham Lincoln was elected president. Kansas would soon enter the Union as a free state. The mixture of emotions was a cauldron, for those who supported Lincoln knew that his election was not popular in the South. In fact, he did not receive a single electoral vote from the South. There were rumblings. Lincoln's life was threatened, immediately and consistently. As Kansas was preparing to be "moved to the states," South Carolina was moved "out of the states."

South Carolina seceded from the Union. Amid the mutterings and the sidewalk conversations was the question: "Secession…was that allowed?"

Four years of war would yield the answer.

Chapter 15

The Thirty-fourth Star

It was an enthusiastic crowd of nearly 100,000 people that greeted president-elect Abraham Lincoln when he arrived at Kensington Railroad Station in Philadelphia on February 21, 1861. He was escorted to the plush Continental Hotel, where he appeared on a balcony with the city's mayor and addressed the masses. The Declaration of Independence had become more meaningful to the man who was about to assume the responsibility of the nation as it stood on the brink of dissolution. The symbolism of this city at this point in America's history was not lost on Lincoln. The next morning, his first stop was Independence Hall:

> *The* [Assembly] *Room was a patriotic shrine that had been redecorated by the city. The liberty bell sat in the corner on an octagonal pedestal that was decorated with flags and the signers of the Declaration of Independence. A sculpture of George Washington stood near the center of the east wall, flanked by portraits of William Penn and the Marquis de Lafayette. A chair said to have been used by John Hancock during the signing of the Declaration of Independence and a block allegedly used for the first reading of the Declaration stood along the outer walls.*[143]

Called on to address the crowd, the exhausted Lincoln was barely audible as he said, "I am filled with deep emotion at finding myself standing here."[144]

Moments later, he was standing on a platform outside the hall, with his son, Tad, by his side, and he raised the first flag honoring the admission of Kansas as the thirty-fourth state. A breeze caught the flag, and it unfurled beautifully above the cheering crowd. Lincoln had hoped it was a good omen.[145]

He could have used such an omen. The night before, Lincoln had been informed that there was a plot to kill him as he passed through Baltimore to Washington. He tended not to take these threats too seriously, perhaps only because he believed that it could not be prevented and not because he found them unbelievable. For the moment, he chose to be encouraged by the free state of Kansas.

On January 29, 1861, Kansas was at last admitted to the Union. At last, Charles Robinson would be a *real* governor. Kansas came into the Union free *and* Republican. The new party had elected a president and had made inroads all over the North. The South had remained firmly Democratic. Just because most Kansans supported or aligned themselves with the

The seal of the state of Kansas. *Kansas State Historical Society.*

Republicans, however, did not mean that all Republicans were of one accord. One was either a "Lane man" or a "Robinson man," and the two were nearly incompatible.

Robinson, a well-educated physician from Massachusetts who had grown tired of attending to the ill, had gone to the gold fields of California before making Kansas his home. His experiences were varied, and he benefited from them all. He earned his place as the "Washington of Kansas," having been one of the prisoners held in Lecompton in 1856; his loyalty and sacrifice were second to none. Historian Albert Castel provided this description:

In appearance Robinson was "tall, sinewy and bald," with cold blue eyes which some regarded as "keen," others as "rather calculating and furtive." All testified to his "pre-possessing presence," and one observer described him as being "more than ordinarily handsome." Despite his background of squatters' riots and Sharps rifles his manner was quiet and dignified, and he held a tight rein on his emotions. A clear, forceful, and ready writer, he was but an ordinary speaker. His character was austere, his intellect high. He was ambitious, hard-working, and strong-willed. He had tremendous self-pride—a source to him of much strength, but also of much weakness.[146]

Castel called James H. Lane "the most colorful and fascinating personality in the history of Kansas."[147] That might be an understatement. Lane could well be the most colorful personality in all of American politics. Castel continued:

He looked, as one writer expressed it, "like nobody else." He was tall, extremely skinny and bony, yet very strong. His face was sallow and hollow-cheeked, with the "sad, dim eyes of a harlot," wild, matted black hair, and thin saturnine lips curling in a "Mephistophelean leer." He moved about nervously, tirelessly, always on the alert, "like one at bay and apprehensive of detection. His customary costume consisted of overall, a calfskin vest, and a black bearskin overcoat, which he is said to have worn even in summer. Vulgar, tempestuous, of fluctuating courage, and utterly unscrupulous, he was a cynic who posed as a zealot, a demagogue who claimed to be a statesman. His private life was that of a satyr, and he was utterly irreligious except at election time. Then, with much fanfare and a great showing of repentance, he would join the politically influential Methodist Church, only to lapse into his old ways once the votes were tallied. Reproached once too often by a Methodist preacher for backsliding, he exploded: "The Methodist Church may go to hell!"[148]

But Lane could talk. In a time when politics was a chief form of entertainment, Lane was a rock star. He was given to using the expression "Great God!" and referring to himself in the third person. The power of his voice could make men leave their homes and take up arms. It made people believe whatever he wanted them to believe. Castel quoted James Ingalls, who said that Lane could have been a great leader had he possessed "a rudimentary perception of the value of personal character as an element of success in public affairs."[149]

At that time, U.S. senators were still elected by the state legislatures, and this was one of the first duties of the governing body of Kansas. Lane actively campaigned for the job, as he was nearly impoverished by 1861. Lane secured the job, as did Samuel Pomeroy, or "Pom the Pius" as many Kansans called him. The margin of victory was slim.

"Moderates moaned that Kansas had been delivered from slave mongers only to be given to radical abolitionists, one extremist group to another," wrote historian Ronald D. Smith. "George Brown, the editor of the *Kansas State Journal*, had the flag above his building lowered to half-mast."[150]

To the everlasting chagrin of Robinson, Lane's political star would rise with the new president. At the Lincoln home in Springfield, Illinois, before Lincoln took office, news, packages and visitors became a constant, but they were not always pleasant. On November 9, 1860, Lincoln received word that he had been hanged in effigy in Pensacola, Florida. Early in 1861, Mary Lincoln received a Christmas present from South Carolina. It was a painting of Lincoln with a rope around his neck, his feet chained and his body tarred and feathered.[151]

The threats came as thick as the accolades, and Lincoln's friends and associates feared for his safety. These were the days before the Secret Service, and there were few soldiers in Washington. Lane wrote to the president offering his services; he volunteered to recruit a guard to protect the president. The seventy-eight men that Lane found became the "Frontier Guard," and they were stationed in the East Room of the White House until other arrangements could be made for the president's safety.[152]

Lincoln was understandably grateful. Once Lane had ingratiated himself with the chief executive, he made the most of the relationship. Lincoln, an

A beardless Abraham Lincoln as he would have appeared when he visited the Kansas Territory in 1859. *Library of Congress.*

astute judge of character in most cases, said that Lane confounded him. The fiery Kansan always seemed to gain an audience with the chief executive. This gave Lane an advantage over Robinson in that political appointments were the prizes everyone was after, and Lane had the inside track with the president. Historian Albert Castel noted that

> *he enjoyed special consideration from Lincoln and possessed remarkable influence with him. Thus, by the end of April, Lane was handing applications for appointments to Lincoln, who in turn was endorsing them without even reading them. Pomeroy, in contrast, obtained only a comparatively minor share of the patronage, and Conway* [Congressman Martin Conway] *practically none. It was soon apparent to all Kansas politicians, as it was to one disgruntled office seeker, that Lincoln "evidently thinks that Lane is the man for all times" and that "Lane gets anything of the President that he asks for while others go begging."*[153]

One of Robinson's important allies was Thomas Ewing Jr., a lawyer who had moved from Ohio to Leavenworth and opened a law office. Ewing came from an influential and well-connected family. His father,

Thomas Ewing Sr., was "a preeminent real estate lawyer, U.S. senator, cabinet secretary for two presidents, and confidant to presidents of all parties for three decades."[154] It wasn't a president but it was close. His father's connections were such that Ewing was not a political lightweight.

Between the November election and the inauguration of President Lincoln in March 1861, seven states seceded from the Union: South Carolina, Mississippi, Florida, Alabama, Georgia, Louisiana and Texas. Delegates from these states met in Montgomery, Alabama, and formed a government with Jefferson Davis, the former secretary of war and recently resigned senator from Mississippi, as its provisional president. On the same day Davis was sworn in, Charles Robinson was being sworn in as the first governor of the state of Kansas, which had passed through more than six years of turmoil. Rather than ending with statehood, it appeared that the grief might extend to the rest of the nation—wars and rumors of wars. Whatever might happen in the East, however, the immediate problem for Kansas was still Missouri. And Missouri's problem was still Kansas.

War Spreads

Fort Sumter is located on one of the numerous islands around the mouth of Charleston's harbor on the South Carolina coast. As the "fire-eaters" of that state clamored to leave the Union, they took issue with the fact that federal troops continued to occupy the post and decided to occupy it instead. After the bombardment, commanding officer Robert Anderson surrendered. The Kentuckian had the flag lowered, carefully folded and packed with his things. Confederate forces raised their new national flag. In response, President Lincoln called for seventy-five thousand troops to be raised to quash the rebellion, allowing that ninety days should be long enough. The nation had joined the Kansas/Missouri conflict.

The Kansas/Missouri border hardly needed a declaration of war, but it helped. Technically, Missouri was a Union state, having voted to reject secession. In reality, the allegiance of counties, communities and even families varied greatly. The strong Unionist areas tended to be St. Louis and environs heavy with manufacturing, immigration and ties to the East. Much of the area bordering the Missouri River and the agricultural counties that bordered Kansas were more Southern in influence. It is not accurate to say that they were proslavery, though some were. Even though slavery was the cause of the Civil War, it was not necessarily what motivated people to take up arms. This was especially true in the border states, where much of the population had Southern roots but were not necessarily slave owners. Another characteristic distinguishing much of the Southern culture from that of the North was its clannishness. Family connections trumped every other loyalty. For this reason alone, many Missourians who might have stayed with the Union, or at the very least remained neutral, were pushed over the fence by the punitive policies or the actions of one or more misguided men who harmed a relative.

Meanwhile, President Lincoln had his hands full. Virginia, Arkansas, Tennessee and North Carolina had joined the ranks of the seceded states, bringing the total to eleven. It was critical to keep the border states (Maryland, Kentucky and Missouri) in the Union. Congress called for 500,000 troops. On July 21, the army of the new Confederate States of America routed the Union army just a few miles south of the nation's capital. The residents of Washington had gone with buggies and picnic lunches to witness what would surely be an exciting but brief clash. They were horrified at the bloodshed and the sight of their soldiers running for dear life. The public began to understand that this was a real war.

Kansans and Missourians understood. They had been through it all before.

Chapter 16

The Fox and the Lyon

Missouri was a mess. The governor, Claiborne Fox Jackson, wanted Missouri to secede, but there were just enough Unionists to keep the state from doing so. Former governor and Mexican-American War hero Sterling Price chaired a convention urging his fellow citizens to remain in the Union but to also remain neutral in the war. (There seemed to be a faction for every conceivable political belief.) According to historian Scott Price, two factors doomed Missouri to remain a mess throughout the war. First, Governor Jackson was in constant contact with the Confederate government requesting military aid; second, Captain Nathaniel Lyon was sent from Fort Riley to command the St. Louis Arsenal:

> *This harbinger from Kansas was described by his best friend, Dr. William A. Hammond, as "intolerant of opposition, prone to inject the most unpopular opinions at times and places where he knew they would be unwelcome; easily aroused to a degree of anger that was almost insane in its manifestations; narrow-minded, mentally unbalanced, and yet with all this, honest to the core, truthful, intelligent, generous to a fault with those he liked, absolutely moral, attentive to his duties, a strict disciplinarian, and that he was one to trust in emergencies with absolute confidence that he would do what he said he would do, even though he gave up his life for his constancy."*[155]

The arsenal contained sixty thousand Springfield and Enfield rifles, 1.5 million cartridges, forty-five thousand tons of gunpowder and several artillery pieces. The contrary Captain Lyon, who constantly found himself in conflict with superiors, found a kindred spirit in Frank Preston Blair Jr. according to Price.

Blair belonged to one of most influential families in the nation. Lyon could not have found a more useful friend nor, as Price said, one more like himself. "Blair had converted the Republican 'Wide-Awake' electioneering clubs into paramilitary Union units," wrote Price. "These new organizations were composed primarily of Germans [often referred to as Hessians or Dutch], 81 percent of whom voted for Lincoln."[156]

Lyon had quietly gotten permission to arm these units and secretly evacuated the remaining arms to Illinois for safekeeping. In May, Governor Jackson called for a training session of the state guard, to be held in St. Louis near the arsenal. It was a simple request on the surface. Technically, these men were on the same side, although they may not have been. Lyon thought that Claiborne Fox Jackson planned to capture the arsenal and its cache of arms.

In May, cannons arrived from Louisiana for Governor Jackson's camp. William T. Sherman (at the time head of a streetcar company in St. Louis) was a frequent visitor to Lyon's office. The moment he heard that artillery had arrived in the enemy's midst, he offered his services to the United States Army.

The impatient Lyon surrounded the camp on May 10, 1861, and forced it to surrender. Again, this appeared ridiculous and wrong on the surface, because the camp was flying an American flag. His fellow Americans were humiliatingly marched through the streets of St. Louis as prisoners of war. It was providence, thought some, that Captain Lyon was kicked in the stomach by a horse and could not savor the moment of surrender.

The sight of U.S. soldiers and Hessians marching these men through the streets (men who would today be the equivalent of the local National Guard) infuriated citizens, and mob violence erupted. At first, the crowd hurled insults and trash. Then shots were fired, one striking and mortally wounding a company commander. The colonel ordered his men to return fire, and twenty-eight men, women and children were killed. As an onlooker, William T. Sherman threw himself on his son to shield the child from flying bullets.

St. Louis was a mess, too. Entirely because of Frank Blair's political connections, Captain Nathaniel Lyon was promoted to brigadier general of volunteers. General William S. Harney, who had been away when this atrocity had occurred, was totally undermined by Blair. He tried to straighten out affairs and went to Sterling Price to discuss the situation. They compromised that the U.S. troops would not make threatening movements in the state and the state guard would maintain order; the German home guard would be moved out of St. Louis. Blair, however, thought these concessions had gone too far and would hamper his plans. He had Harney removed from command. Once again, the Lincoln patronage won out.

It was time for a little talk with Lyon and Blair. Governor Jackson, his aide and Sterling Price traveled to St. Louis, where a marathon meeting decided absolutely nothing. The meeting came to an abrupt end when Lyon said, "Rather than concede to the State of Missouri for one single instant, the right to dictate to my government in any matter however important, I would see you, you, and you, and every man, woman, and child in the state dead and buried. This means war. In one hour one of my officers will call and conduct you out of my lines."[157]

The men did not wait for Lyon's escort but instead got aboard a train for Jefferson City. They stopped periodically for water and to cut the telegraph lines, as well as to burn the bridges on the Gasconade and the Osage Rivers. Jackson was referred to as the "valiant bridge burning fugitive Governor."[158]

Even Unionists were appalled by the events in St. Louis. As Lyon and his command pursued Jackson, the Missouri legislature mobilized the state guard, placing it under the command of Sterling Price. Governor Jackson also called for fifty thousand men to repel the "invasion" of federal troops. Due to the weakness of Price's forces, he sought support from Confederates in Arkansas.

Back in Kansas, Governor Robinson considered Governor Jackson's actions to be synonymous with a declaration of war. After all, the presence of federal troops would not necessarily merit the word "invasion." On June 17, 1861, he urged Kansans to prepare for attack. Militia units were formed up and down the border. The First and Second Kansas Volunteers were sent to join General Lyon.[159]

Once in June and twice in July 1861, Charles "Doc" Jennison raided western Missouri. Riding with Jennison in that initial raid were one hundred Mound City Sharps Rifle Guards, supposedly requested by the military in Kansas City but in reality organized under no authority. As Jennison rode around the countryside generally bullying people, word of his actions spread to the *real* authorities, who ordered him out of the state. Somehow on his forays, Jennison seemed to accumulate slaves, who accompanied him back to Kansas, a redeeming quality to some and another example of overstepping his authority to others.

On July 4, Jennison made the ultimate patriotic move, capturing a wagon train of military supplies headed to Fort Arbuckle. Major Samuel D. Sturgis had been protecting the train, though obviously not effectively. Captain William E. Prince ordered Jennison to return the wagons "intact."

The captain generously interpreted the actions in the best possible light and wrote that "the men had taken the train had acted with…the best motives for the interests of the country and ignorant of the degree of criminality attached to the offense." However, Captain Prince added that such acts, not sanctioned by the proper authorities, would be considered privateering and were punishable by death.[160]

In the meantime, General Lyon was determined to bring General Price to bay. On August 10, 1861, the Union forces under Lyon collided with Confederates under General Ben McCulloch and the Missouri State Guard under Sterling Price at Wilson's Creek, Missouri. From McCulloch's report to the War Department in Richmond:

> *I have the honor to report that the enemy 12,000 strong, attacked us at daylight this morning. Although they were superior in discipline and arms and had gained a strong position, we have repulsed them and gained a decided victory. The enemy fled before us at 1 o'clock, after eight hours' hard fighting, leaving many dead and wounded and prisoners.*
>
> *Six pieces of cannon were taken and many small-arms. Among the dead we found General Lyon, and sent his body to his successor this evening. The loss was also severe on our side.*[161]

The tone of Union officer Colonel Franz Sigel was much more somber as he reported to Major General John C. Frémont:

> *I respectfully report to you that after a battle fought 10 miles south of Springfield…between our forces and the rebel army, and in which General Lyon was killed, I have taken temporarily the command of the Union troops… It was found necessary to retreat towards Rolla…The enemy's forces cannot be less than 20,000 men…Once in possession of Springfield, the enemy will be able to raise the southwest of the state against us, add a*

great number of men to his army, make Springfield a great depot…I do not see the probability of making an effective resistance without reinforcement of not less than 5,000 men, infantry, one or two regiments of cavalry, and at least two batteries.[162]

The First Kansas Volunteers lost 284 of 800 engaged, a staggering loss. The Second Kansas lost 70 of 600. Lyon was shot while ordering the Second Kansas and two Iowa regiments forward. The loss of General Lyon, the man arguably responsible for all of this bloodshed, would be oddly significant. Like John Brown, he was more valuable dead than alive. Historian Scott Price noted:

Lyon provided the Union with the martyr and heroic figure it so desperately needed to rally the northern people to continue the growing struggle against a foe who would prove wily, resourceful, valiant and difficult to defeat—their fellow Americans. Eventually it became clear that that he had not sacrificed his life in vain, nor had he sold it cheaply. Lyon died in the manner that he would have wanted: leading his men into a typhoon of steel in a desperate charge. All things considered, he was not defeated at all; he was merely killed.[163]

Lyon had been a general less than three months. Through the actions of one vain officer, it was not just a family or community that was pushed to the other side; it was also an entire army. The impact on Missouri and Kansas was disastrous.

Chapter 17

The War Chieftain

War sometimes presents some wonderful opportunities. It certainly did for Senator Jim Lane, who was determined to be the "war chieftan of Kansas."[164]

His only obstacle in this pursuit was Governor Charles Robinson, who had the position of commander and chief over the state militia, as well as the authority to raise regiments to be placed under federal control. But Lane had the trump card: President Abraham Lincoln.

The president addressed Secretary of War Simon Cameron on June 20, 1861, concerning Lane:

> *We need the services of such a man out there at once; that we better appoint him a brigadier general of volunteers to-day, and send him off with such authority to raise a force (I think two regiments better than three, but as to this I am not particular) as you think will get him into actual work quicker. Tell him when he starts to put it through not to be writing or telegraphing back here, but put it through.*[165]

If Governor Robinson was taken aback by the fact that Jim Lane was usurping his authority to raise troops, he must have been beside himself to learn that Lincoln had also made Lane a brigadier general. The silver lining for Robinson was the fact that it was illegal for Lane to be both a U.S. senator *and* a general. Robinson assumed that accepting the commission had necessarily caused Lane's Senate seat to be vacated, so naturally the governor appointed one of his friends, Frederick Stanton, to take his place.

Lane said that he had never actually *accepted* the commission as a general, despite numerous newspaper articles to the contrary. Apparently, the commission was offered to him, but when he realized that it would cost him his Senate seat, he declined to do anything. He did not intend to leave the Senate, and he also had every intention of commanding troops.

"In the weeks to follow," wrote historian Albert Castel, "he became the first and probably the only man ever to command large numbers of United States troops without legal authority from the Federal Government."[166]

Lane chose a location near Fort Scott to set up his command. Dubbed "Fort Lincoln," the quickly constructed outpost in many ways presented a clear picture of the entire war effort to that time—thrown together from available materials.

More than the Missourians themselves, Governor Robinson feared Lane. The governor wrote to General John C. Frémont expressing his fear that Lane's forces would "get up a war by going over the line, committing depredations, and then returning to our State." Further, Robinson asked Frémont to "relieve us of the Lane Brigade, [and] I will guarantee Kansas from invasion from Missouri."[167]

While Robinson stewed over Lane, the firebrand grabbed attention, headlines and support. One valid reason for this support among abolitionists was the large number of slaves "liberated" (or "stolen," depending on the point of view). Lane had claimed that slavery could not survive the Union army and set about demonstrating that fact in Missouri. Each time he raided the state, scores of blacks followed him out.[168] "By the time the brigade completed its march [Autumn 1861], scores of Negroes were present in its ranks as teamsters and cooks and even as soldiers," wrote Albert Castel.[169]

Lane's liberation of slaves served a twofold purpose for him: it hurt the enemy economically, and it lent an appearance of purity to his motives for making war. If it was all about freedom, then any means of making war was acceptable.

Chapter 18

The Problem with Slavery

The people with the most to gain from the Civil War had the least power to do anything about it.

It was estimated that 4 million blacks were held in bondage in America at the time. It is difficult for most people to imagine exactly what slavery meant. In his opening to *The Civil War*, that magnificent documentary production for PBS, Ken Burns wrote an eloquent script for David McCullough's rich voice. With images of cotton fields in the background, McCullough described the day of a slave—backbreaking labor from sunup to sundown. That, however, was not the problem with slavery.

Most white people at the time lived the same way. The luxurious life of Scarlett O'Hara from *Gone With the Wind* was true for only an extremely small percentage of Southerners, or Northerners for that matter. Most of the population, in order to survive, worked from sunup to sundown. The problem with slavery can be summed up in that word tossed around by the Founding Fathers: self-determination. In a modern society where people are free to move from one job to the next and from one city to the next, to marry and divorce and marry over and over and to have children with or without the benefit of marriage, citizens of twenty-first-century America arguably have more self-determination than any generation before.

People leave dead-end jobs every day. People call in sick and goof off. Feeling unappreciated and unloved is grounds for divorce. Anyone desiring a new start can move to the other side of town or to the other coast. Imagine having no control over the most basic of decisions—when to get up, where to live and who to marry. Imagine not being *allowed* to learn to read. Imagine your son, ten years old, sold. Imagine your wife, the mother of your children and the center of your world, sold with no more thought than one would trade cars today. Imagine falling into bed every night, bone weary, knowing that tomorrow would be exactly the same and that a thousand tomorrows would be the same for your children. Imagine that this is your life and the lives of your family, your friends and your neighbors. Imagine that no matter what you do or how hard you try, nothing will change. That kind of oppression kills the human spirit. *That* is the problem with slavery.

The situations between slaves and masters were as varied as the people themselves, and no blanket statement could cover them all—except

Battle flag of the First Kansas Colored, with names of the battles in which the men participated. These men were the first black troops to be organized and see battle after the Civil War began. James H. Lane did not wait for permission from Washington to form the unit. *Kansas State Historical Society.*

that no one wished to be enslaved. Not every slave owner was evil, not every slave was beaten or molested and there is great evidence of bonds between some slaves and their owners. That being said, there was, and is, no excuse for slavery. The opening of the Kansas Territory was a glimmer of hope that one day soon a generation of black people could be born free in America.

In August 1862, the First Kansas Colored Regiment was formed by the controversial Senator James H. Lane, and blacks could have a say in their own fate. Historian Bryce Benedict noted:

> The fact that the United States was not accepting black troops was of little consequence to Lane. He managed to get them clothed and armed by the government, and they fought a successful engagement against Missouri guerillas in October 1862, well before the regiment was accepted into U.S. Service in January, 1863.[170]

Many of the men of the First Kansas were, of course, Missourians—slaves who had escaped, perhaps through the efforts of Jim Lane. The Fifty-fourth Massachusetts has received much acclaim because of its portrayal in the movie *Glory*, leading to the popular belief that it was the first regiment of African Americans organized during the war. That distinction, however, belongs to the First Kansas Colored. These men were also the first to see battle and the first to die in action, according to the Kansas State Historical Society. A detachment of 225 men faced twice that many Confederates at Island Mound in Bates County, Missouri. There were ten men from the First Kansas killed in the battle and another twelve wounded. There were other battles to follow, and in each one, the men of the First Kansas Colored demonstrated that they were at least equal to any white soldier.

OSCEOLA

For years, raids were conducted back and forth across the Kansas/Missouri border. But when Osceola, Missouri, a town of fewer than fifty homes, was struck by Jayhawkers in September 1861, it became the rallying cry for Confederate guerillas to retaliate. What was so different about Osceola?

As historian Bryce Benedict wrote, "Osceola should have been an inconsequential target, but it was a commercial landing on the Osage River and now it was rumored to be a depot for [General Sterling] Price's army."[171]

Perhaps it was the "potential" in itself that Osceola would serve as a staging area for Price's invasion of Missouri more than any other factor that led the Kansas officers' decision to burn the town. Among the reasons given was "that it was traitorous to the core." That would not have set Osceola apart from dozens of other communities. But another reason was "that the enemy intended to make of it, during the winter, a military post" and "that it was a strong position, and could be easily fortified." Colonels James Montgomery and John Ritchie decided to torch the town. Colonel William Weer was opposed.

"With the exception of Morristown earlier that month, at no time previous in this war had the combatants burned enemy towns," wrote Benedict. "The occupants of Osceola had every reason to believe that although there might be some thievery visited upon them, and even perhaps selected buildings destroyed, the persons and homes of the general population would be spared. Their shock must have been awful as they learned the decision had been made to burn the town."[172]

In one of those nonsensical ironies that characterized the war in Kansas and Missouri, Montgomery agreed with burning the town, yet he ordered that a tannery be spared, as well as residences on the outskirts of town. That way, the women and children would have a place to take refuge.[173] The burning of Osceola had a far greater general impact than on the homeless residents created by it, however. It was a milestone in the escalation of violence on the border. Historian Albert Castel reasoned that one-third to one-half of the people living in western Missouri were either Unionists or at least neutral and that raids led by Lane and Jennison had turned many of them into Confederates.

Not to be outdone, Confederate forces revisited Humboldt. The small raid in September had been but a foreshadowing of what was to come. The militia stationed in Humboldt had made its rounds and returned home, finding no rebels about and believing the neighborhood to be safe. Shortly afterward, more than three hundred Confederate horsemen easily took the unsuspecting men prisoner. Colonel Talbot, commanding the regular force, was assisted by bushwhacker Tom Livingston. One citizen was shot and killed, and then the town was torched. The townspeople managed to save a few of their buildings, but most of the town was destroyed. There were also reports that some of the rebels helped women remove furniture or valuables from their homes before they were consumed by the conflagration. The raiding party also visited the countryside south of Humboldt.[174]

That same month, Missourians pillaged Linn County, and three men were killed; Dick Yeager, leading about twenty guerillas, raided the village of Gardner, Kansas. On December 12, 1861, Major H.H. Williams of Montgomery's command burned Papinsville and Butler, Missouri.

"[V]irtually every town and hamlet and a multitude of farms in western Missouri had experienced a raid or suffered outrageous intimidation," wrote historian Don Gilmore. "The Jayhawkers had become a pox, and everywhere they traveled or stopped, for a radius of several miles in every direction, the area became blighted or despoiled. The people, whether living in town or in the country, now lived in a state of continual terror."[175]

As 1861 dissolved into 1862, events in the East grabbed the headlines: the Battle of Manassas, Virginia, or Bull Run, was a Confederate victory and earned General Thomas J. Jackson the name "Stonewall." President Lincoln's blockade of the South also created hardships and animosity. But for residents of the Kansas/Missouri border, the war was much closer—in their neighborhoods and homes. Both sides of the border lived in constant fear of being robbed, murdered or burned out.

Surely the government or the military commanders would find some way to keep private citizens safe in 1862.

Chapter 19

The Enigma

In 1862, Kansas learned the name of William Clarke Quantrill, and they would never forget it.

He had a fair complexion, fine features and a good mind. His morals and motives have been debated since his name became infamous in the border war. There is almost no quality that Quantrill (sometimes Quantrell) was said to have possessed that someone else had not described as the very opposite. Perhaps, even at the time, he was an enigma.

The young schoolteacher headed west to help support his widowed mother. Looking to the Kansas Territory, as did so many other folks from Ohio, he came to Kansas in 1857 in the company of two neighbors. He helped work their claim. There is little doubt from his adventures that he possessed some wanderlust and ambition. He joined an expedition to Utah led by General Albert Sidney Johnston. He was hired on as a teamster. In the spring, he mined for gold, one of the fortune seekers who hoped to find the mother lode at Pikes Peak.

Worn and weary, he came back to Kansas to teach school. The numerous letters to his mother reflect a youth searching for his way in the world. He had seen death, feared death and been close to death. He told his mother of hard times past and hard times on the horizon. More than one note of melancholy is found in his writings.[176]

Coming from the free state of Ohio, one would assume that young Quantrill's personal and political leanings would reflect those liberal views. Perhaps they did at first; perhaps his outlook was altered by events he

This image of William Clarke Quantrill is inscribed for Lydia from Quantrill, 1860. He gave it to Lydia Stone, whose family had a hotel in Lawrence, after she nursed him during an illness. He personally protected the Stones during his raid on Lawrence. *Emory A. Cantey Jr., www. canteymyerscollection.com.*

observed. He certainly was familiar with the exploits of John Brown and was appalled that a murderer had been held up as a hero and martyr. At some point, he determined to take the side of the proslavery faction, although by outward appearances he portrayed himself as an abolitionist. He was a party to a raid to free slaves at the home of Morgan Walker, located in Jackson County, Missouri. Quantrill reportedly went to Walker and told him that the raid would occur, leading his partners into an ambush. From this time forward, there was no turning back.[177]

Quantrill was staying with friends in Blue Springs, Missouri, which had been relatively spared from the border warfare of the territorial days. That was about to change. In the autumn of 1861, Quantrill heard of Jayhawking a few miles north of the community. Quantrill and others, under the leadership of Andrew Walker, went after the outlaws. Albert Castel noted:

> *Walker's party tracked them to the Strawder Stone farm, which had been plundered and set afire. Mrs. Stone ran up to them and showed where one of the jayhawkers had struck her on the head with a pistol. Now thoroughly enraged, they continued on rapidly to the Billy Thompson farm one-half mile beyond. Here they came upon the marauders just as they were leaving the burning house and were preparing to mount their horses. Walker and his men charged immediately, opening fire as they did so.*

Their bullets killed the man who had hit Mrs. Stone, but the rest of the Kansans escaped into Independence.[178]

What one would expect to be the logical outcome of this situation is certainly not what happened next. Strawder Stone and one of his men were arrested for murder. Quantrill went to the justice of the peace and swore that he had committed the shooting. His friends were released, and oddly enough, no charges were filed against Quantrill. But the Unionist militia were not so easily satisfied and made it known they would bring him to justice.[179]

"This selfless act made Quantrill a hero in the area," wrote Donald Gilmore.[180]

It was during this time that Andrew Walker withdrew from the group, and Quantrill followed him as the leader of this small band. According to Albert Castel, these men formed Quantrill's first squad. Some of their names would be almost as widely known as his: Bill Hallar, Jim and John Little, Ed and John Koger, Harrison Trace, Joe Gilchrist, Bill Gregg, Joe Vaughn and George Todd. Soon they were joined by Ol' Shepherd, George Maddox, Perry Hoy and Fletch Taylor.[181]

On more than one occasion, Quantrill would display qualities that would be considered "redeeming," had his enemies been generous enough to acknowledge them. One such incident occurred in December 1861, when a "renegade Southern soldier" named George Searcy began stealing horses and mules in the neighborhood, from Southerners and Unionists alike. Quantrill's men captured and hanged him and then returned the stolen goods to their owners.[182]

Quantrill's reputation grew. On March 7, 1862, he and his band rode into the village of Aubrey, tucked just inside the Kansas state line south of Kansas City. Renting a room in the village tavern was Abraham Ellis, who had been the superintendent of schools at Stanton when Quantrill was a teacher. Awakened by the shouts of frightened guests, Ellis naturally ran to the window of his second-floor room to see what was happening. At that moment, Quantrill wheeled his horse and fired his revolver. The bullet smashed the glass and went into Ellis's forehead.

Quantrill soon arrived in the tavern, and unbelievably, the bloody Ellis staggered downstairs. Quantrill was aghast that he had shot his friend and washed the blood from his face himself. Ellis recovered, but the wound was visible between his eyes for the rest of his life, a macabre testament to Quantrill's marksmanship.[183]

In *Dark Command*, Walter Pidgeon plays "Cantrell," a schoolteacher turned guerrilla obviously based on the exploits of William Clarke Quantrill. In this episode, Cantrell's murderous ways are stopped by his own mother, who kills him. *Author's collection. Republic Pictures.*

According to Albert Castel (and others have concurred over the years), "Quantrill instinctively realized the essence of guerrilla warfare: stay always on the offensive, striking first here and then there, and never giving the enemy a chance to concentrate his forces against you."[184]

Several days after Aubrey, Quantrill and his men attacked a Union garrison at Liberty; he maintained control of his men and allowed no looting, which was appreciated by the pro-Southern residents. They made the band welcome.[185] Their reception at Liberty was exactly the problem. It was impossible to catch guerrillas if they were supported by the civilian population.

What happened next may have seemed like a logical step for the federal government, which had lost all control of the border. On March 13, 1862, General Henry Halleck issued General Order No. 2. Aimed at putting an end to guerrilla violence, it had the opposite effect. It specified that men of partisan units would be considered outlaws and subject to execution. Three weeks later, Confederate president Jefferson Davis signed the CSA Partisan Ranger Act, which gave the status of legitimate military units to those in the field.

News of Halleck's order spread like wildfire. Missouri, which had voted to remain loyal to the Union, had felt the heavy hand of the federal government from August 1861, when General Frémont had established martial law in the state. Lincoln later authorized General Halleck to suspend habeas corpus, thereby allowing citizens to be imprisoned without charges. Halleck later issued orders that stated that anyone sabotaging a railroad would be shot and that "disloyal citizens" had to pay thousands in levies of personal property. This initiated wholesale looting by federal troops.

In May 1862, Major General Schofield finally got to the point where he said that guerrillas were to be shot on the spot. Two months later, he went a step further and ordered that all able-bodied men should join the Union forces or be considered Southern sympathizers and thus traitors.

The military leadership had succeeded in leaving its citizens no way to remain neutral and had ensured that guerrillas had nothing to lose. Albert Castel noted:

> *Hundreds of pro-Southern Missourians who so far had taken no active part in the war, now suddenly found themselves called on to fight against their friends and relatives. Rather than do this, they either went into hiding or else joined up with Porter, Poindexter, Quantrill, or some other partisan leader. In addition, many ex-members of Price's army, men who had been allowed to return home with the assurance that they would not be required to serve in the Union Army, felt that this promise had been violated and hence took to the bush. As a consequence, the strength and number of the guerrilla bands increased enormously.*[186]

Castel also commented that Schofield's order was effective in mobilizing true Missouri Unionists to meet the challenge of the Southerners. Everyone was armed and ready to do battle. As conditions worsened in western Missouri, many rightly or wrongly blamed Kansas.

It was hard to ignore the significance of Fort Leavenworth. Troops were stationed there, orders were issued from the post and justice was meted out. Perry Hoy, one of the guerrillas who had been with Quantrill from the beginning of the war, was being held at Fort Leavenworth awaiting a death sentence. Quantrill hoped to exchange him for a Union officer—Lieutenant Levi Copeland, captured at the Battle of Lone Jack, Missouri.[187] Unfortunately for all involved, circumstance did not work out that way. Donald Gilmore quoted the August 1, 1862 newspaper account of Hoy's execution:

> *The prisoner* [Hoy] *was marched on to the grounds by the soldiers; he wore a black suit and a felt hat; his arms were pinioned. Hoy was brought to the place where he was to be shot, made to kneel and his hat removed. A detachment of soldiers stood about twenty yards distant, and the moment the guard left, the command to fire was given—twelve volumes of fire leap*[t] *from the rifles, and Hoy* [was] *dead. He fell over upon his face and died without a struggle. One ball went through his head and two through his body…*[H]*e was placed in a coffin and borne to the military burial ground. The soldiers marched off, the band playing a lively air.*[188]

When Quantrill read this account, he scribbled a command to one of his men: "Take Lieutenant Copeland out and shoot him. Go to Woodsmall's camp [?], get two prisoners from his camp, shoot them, and return as quickly as possible."[189] The orders were promptly carried out.

Quantrill then ordered his men to saddle their horses. They were headed to Kansas. En route, they killed 10 men who just happened to be in the wrong place at the wrong time. When they reined their horses at the outskirts of Olathe, Quantrill ordered 60 of his roughly 140 men to cordon the town so no one could escape. At the courthouse square, 125 militiamen stood to defend the town, until they saw the guerrillas. The raiders walked behind their horses, using them as shields, drew their guns and demanded the surrender of the militia. One can imagine how these heavily armed, seasoned combat veterans appeared to this citizen militia. They put up their hands to surrender, except for one, who was promptly shot.[190]

That made fourteen men in payment for the life of Perry Hoy.

Chapter 20

City of Sorrow

In Oak Hill Cemetery, Lawrence, Kansas, there is a rather large and impressive monument that was erected in 1895 to the memory of those killed in this town on August 21, 1863. It bears only one name: Quantrell.

This frequent misspelling of the guerrilla's name appears throughout accounts from the day, as well as on gravestones. It would be a safe bet that no other name appears on so many grave markers in Kansas. The monument instructs those interested in finding the names of the citizens who were killed to visit the Douglas County Clerk's office or the Kansas State Historical Society. On the hilltop, there are other grave markers that tell the story—these unfortunate people died during Quantrill's raid. The grave of Senator/General James Lane is nearby. It is rather ironic; he did not die in the raid, yet his name was first on the death list carried by the men who appeared on this very hilltop in 1863. The guerrillas arrived at 5:00 a.m., and the sleeping city lay at their feet. Some removed the blue shirts they had worn to disguise their identity. Others checked revolvers or cinched their saddles.

Lawrence, Kansas, had been the focal point of rage for many Missourians since the territorial days. Though Topeka was now the official capital of the state, Lawrence remained the de facto abolitionist capital. It was the home of both Jim Lane and Charles Robinson, and the policies for raids into Missouri came from Lawrence if not the actual orders. Historian Albert Castel noted that "the town represented to them all they hated and feared in Kansas. It was the citadel of abolitionism. It was the home of Jim Lane. It was the headquarters of the Red Legs. And its numerous well-stocked stores, rich banks, and fine homes offered tempting targets."[191]

Those fine homes and goods were tempting for a multitude of reasons. While some of Quantrill's men may have sought to enrich themselves by the raid, they believed that the prosperity of Lawrence had come by the sacrifice of communities in western Missouri. "Remember Osceola!" was a frequent cry of the rebels, as was "Butler!" and, sometimes, "Jennison!"

Quantrill had held a council of war among his most trusted lieutenants. They shared his sentiments about Lawrence but not his optimism. It was a suicide mission. But Quantrill had thought through every aspect of the raid. He had sent scouts into the town. John Noland, a free black, and Fletch Taylor had observed that the town had poor defenses and was ripe for such an attack.[192]

The recollections of Cole Younger indicate not only the events but also the motives for striking Lawrence:

> *Disguised as a cattle trader, Lieutenant Fletcher Taylor...spent a week at the Eldridge house in Lawrence, Kansas, from which place had gone out the Jayhawkers who in three months just previous had slain 200 men and boys, taken many women prisoners, and stolen no one knows how many horses...The lieutenant's report was encouraging. The city itself was poorly garrisoned; the camp beyond was not formidable; the streets were wide.*
>
> *"You have heard the report," said Quantrell when the lieutenant finished. "It is a long march; we march through soldiers. We attack soldiers; we must retreat through soldiers. What shall it be? Speak out, Anderson!"*
>
> *"Lawrence or hell," replied Anderson, instantly. With fire flashing in his eyes as he recalled the recent wreck from which his sister had been taken in Kansas City, he added: "But with one proviso, that we kill every male thing."*
>
> *"Todd?" called Quantrell.*
>
> *"Lawrence, if I knew not a man would get back alive."*
>
> *"Gregg?" This was Capt. William Gregg who still lives in Kansas City, one of the bravest men that ever faced powder, an in action the coolest, probably, in the entire command.*
>
> *"Lawrence," he replied. "It is the home of Jim Lane; the nurse of Jayhawkers.*

"Jarrette?"

"Lawrence, by all means," my brother-in-law answered. "It is the head devil of the killing and burning in Jackson county. I vote to fight it and with fire—burn it before we leave."

Shepherd, Dick Maddox, so on, Quantrell called the roll.

"Have you all voted?" shouted Quantrell.

There was no word.

"Then Lawrence it is; saddle up."[193]

How on earth would they get to Lawrence undetected? They would just trot their horses over the state line, just south of Aubrey.

The site of Quantrill's first raid into the state was no longer defenseless. Captain Joshua Pike commanded Company K, Ninth Kansas Volunteer

This depiction of a guerrilla raid left easterners with an image of barbaric hordes on the Kansas/ Missouri border. *Kansas State Historical Society.*

Cavalry, and Company D, Eleventh Kansas Volunteer Cavalry, and had one hundred cavalrymen at his disposal, on paper anyway. Pike later said that he only had twenty-eight able to fight. Even with a full force, Pike's assessment that he would not have been able to stop them and that it would have been suicide was certainly accurate. He did send a courier to his commander as the word of the invasion spread. That was at about 5:00 p.m.[194]

Some of Quantrill's men wore blue uniforms, and when they were questioned by Union soldiers in the village of Gardner, the raiders said that they were federal cavalry headed to Lawrence to have their horses shod.[195] As it became darker, Quantrill was forced to recruit local guides in order to stay on the main body of the road and thus on time. The guides were killed when they were no longer useful. Historian Don Gilmore noted:

> At the home of Joseph Stone, a refugee Missourian, Stone was recognized as the man who had caused [George] Todd to be arrested in Kansas City early in the war. Todd wished to kill Stone but Quantrill thought the noise would alarm the area. Todd understood, sent for a rope to hang him. When none could be found, a musket was brought instead. Todd made short work of Stone, beating his brains out.[196]

Albert Castel told slightly a different version:

> Todd thereupon took a Sharps carbine and commanded Sam Clifton, a new member of the gang whose loyalty was suspected, to club Stone to death. Young Frank Smith became so sick as he watched Clifton carry out the horrible order that he nearly fell of his horse.[197]

The column of troops rode on through the darkness. Quantrill was concerned about the time. They had to arrive by dawn.

For some residents of Lawrence, the destruction of 1856 was fresh in their minds. For others, it was distant history, having occurred before they arrived. There were rumors that Quantrill would strike, but as is often the case with guerrilla warfare, the elusive Quantrill was blamed for every outrage within hundreds of miles. There were multiple warnings of raids that turned into false alarms.

Sarah Fitch certainly thought so. The housewife described the night of August 20, 1863: "E. [Edward Fitch, her husband] and I walked home together—going down the whole length of our principal business street speaking of all the new buildings & all the projected improvements—How bright—how glowing with happiness and prosperity seemed the future."[198]

On the morning of the twenty-first, mist clung to the Kansas River bottoms and glowed faint pink and orange as the sun rose. It would be another hot day, and one of those rare days in Kansas with no wind. Sarah Fitch began stirring and preparing for the day. Some of her neighbors were still sleeping when the peaceful morning was splintered by gunfire.

At the south end of town, twenty-one men of the Fourteenth Kansas were encamped and still asleep. They were poorly armed, and many of their weapons were being repaired. One camp was located across the Kansas River (the north side of town) at the ferry crossing. The partisan rangers rode through the camp and dispatched the unprepared soldiers as quickly as it could be described. There was a camp of the Second Colored Regiment, also about twenty men, but they were segregated and farther away, a prejudice that served them well on this day as they had time to flee and would have been shot down on the spot, noted Lieutenant Colonel (retired) Ed Kennedy, who often leads the Lawrence Staff Ride for various military personnel. Any military defenses the town would have counted on were gone in seconds after the raid started.

"I was awakened…By the rapid discharge of firearms on Massachusetts Street," wrote State Provost Marshal Alexander Banks, as quoted in *Black Flag*. "I arose and looked down from the window. I saw a body of horsemen riding rapidly up the street toward the hotel…I told my wife that the guerrillas had taken the town."[199]

The guerrillas knew exactly where to go:

> *The guerrillas entered Lawrence diagonally, from southeast to northwest, crossing vacant lots and avoiding obstacles. At Quincy and Rhode Island Streets, according to a preconceived plan, some of the guerrillas left the column to form a cordon around the town. Another detachment of eleven headed to Mount Oread, a high, then-barren hill, overlooking the town that gave a perfect view to the east for fifteen miles. They were to report any approaching Federals.*[200]

The largest body of Quantrill's men rode down Massachusetts Street, the main thoroughfare. They did, indeed, "have the town," and they would keep it for four long hours. Historian Noble Prentis summed up the attack:

There was first the hurried murder of the charge, the guerillas firing on whoever they saw as they rode past, and afterward the deliberate and painstaking massacre, house by house, and man by man...As is often the case in seasons of terror, as in shipwrecks, the women displayed the highest courage, struggling with their bare hands to save their houses from the flames, their sons and husbands from the swarming murderers. The town was robbed and burned, the black smoke rising in a great cloud in the still air. The Eldridge House, the successor of the old Free State Hotel, burned in 1856, was specially devoted to flames. The safeguard given the guests and inmates of this hotel by Quantrill himself, was the one ray of mercy that illuminated the darkness of the time.[201]

One example of a woman's bravery was that of Kate Riggs, who grabbed the reins of a guerrilla's horse and kept jerking it away as he tried to shoot her husband. Sam Riggs was able to escape because of his wife's heroics. Others were not so fortunate. Sadly, the experience of Sarah Fitch was not isolated. Two weeks after the raid, she found the strength to write to her in-laws of her husband's death:

Ed Fitch was murdered by Quantrill's raiders in his parlor in the presence of his wife and children, and then his home burned with the body still in it. *Kansas State Historical Society.*

[A]ll at once twenty or thirty of them swept up to the house, surrounded it, and in an instant, a ruffian, a demon burst open—oh that face! It haunts me day & night, a coarse, brutal, blood thirsty face—inflamed with hellish passions & strong drink for he was evidently intoxicated—with horrid oaths he said that not one of us should leave (he had not seen E. then) another one was behind with perhaps one spark more of humanity in his bosom & he said "let the women & children go"—I was almost beside myself with terror for Edward—I knew his doom was sealed—that demon—who was there swearing—shouting—screaming—in our dear little parlor, with his revolver cocked in one hand—the matches lit to fire our home in the other—I felt there was no mercy there—oh my friends— do you wonder that in that instant—(for all passed much more quickly than I can write it)—that my heart almost stopped its beating—and in utter despair, I almost doubted if there was a God who loved us—He that witch—turned & saw my Edward—oh Mother—so calm so self possessed—and without a word the deadly aim was taken—shot after shot in rapid succession—emptying his own revolver, then taking the weapon from the hand of his companion, and using all its load to make sure work of death—oh can you picture that moment—I begged, I implored—I looked around on that circle of hard cruel faces—and I knew there was no help—no help—oh had God forgotten us—the match was applied to our house—I pleaded, I begged thrice to take him out—not to burn that precious body—But with an oath, a terrible oath—he pointed his pistol to my breast & said he would shoot me too if I didn't leave—& I took my screaming children—& went across the road & threw ourselves on the grass—how did I live—I know not…

[F]or the children's sake I try to keep a cheerful face—for Julie says—"Mama why do you cry! Isn't papa in Heaven with God?" and "don't he love us now just the same as he used to?"[202]

Prentis was accurate in stating that the raiders methodically went from house to house. They carried a list of targets, with Jim Lane at the top. Lane managed to escape to a cornfield in his nightshirt. Charles Robinson, also on the list, watched the entire raid unfold from his barn. Undiscovered and helpless, one can only imagine his horror while wondering the fate of his wife and his friends. Prentis was accurate, too, in indicating that not all of the actions of the raiders were heinous.

Brooklyn was a growing village in Douglas County at the intersection of the Santa Fe Trail and the Military Road. Following the raid on Lawrence, Quantrill's men came through and burned the town. It was never rebuilt. *Author's collection.*

Missourians torched houses but helped women carry out their furniture. One lady arrived home to find her house in ashes but family photos under a tree in the yard. Estimates of the dead range from 150 to 200 men. No women were killed, and there were no reported instances of rape.[203]

The Lawrence Massacre has been called a "wholesale slaughter," but it certainly was not, and is remarkable in that regard. With nearly every business burned, and more than one hundred homes, the devastation in dollars was more than $2 million, a staggering amount in that era. But considering that there were at least 350 guerrillas, who by the very definition are not accustomed to taking orders or following military discipline, the number of dead could have been so much worse. Just a glance at the numbers indicate that not every man with Quantrill took a life. Knowing that some, like Bloody Bill Anderson (who murdered 14 men according to Cole Younger), took more than one life, that leaves even more guerrillas who managed some restraint. George Todd had evidenced his capacity to inflict punishment on the way to Lawrence.

Many of these men were veterans of other raids, and some had been the victims of Jayhawking atrocities. None were strangers to violence, and had they not shown mercy or lacked the stomach for killing, the town of 3,000 could have been totally destroyed.[204]

As historian Greg Hildreth commented, "One of the things that struck me about the war in this area is the constant contradiction between the abject violence and their Victorian sense of proper behavior and chivalrous manners...They would murder a man suspected of Union sympathy and burn his home and farm, but insist that his wife go unharmed...that is just ludicrous to me."[205]

One of those "ludicrous" moments occurred at the hotel owned by Nathan Stone. Quantrill had been a guest there years before and remembered that Stone's wife and daughter had cared for him. He ordered them and their property be spared and set up his headquarters there. So, while his men wreaked unspeakable revenge on this town, he enjoyed a leisurely breakfast and reminisced about old times with his hosts.[206] Other raiders stopped for breakfast or helped themselves to the stores of goods, gorging on canned oysters or ice cream and helping themselves to any whiskey that was available.

The guerrillas—many drunk and loaded with plunder—headed south out of town and crossed the Wakarusa River at Blanton's Bridge. They tried to set fire to the bridge behind them but it wouldn't catch. They burned farms along the way. Much of the plunder was tossed aside as the horses, many ready to drop, struggled to climb out of the Wakarusa River Valley. By this time, more than one thousand federal soldiers were in pursuit. They caught up at Brooklyn, a village at the intersection of the Santa Fe Trail and the Military Road. The rebels torched Brooklyn and repelled their pursuers. A second encounter would take place just outside Paola, and again the rebels kept the soldiers at bay long enough to get back across the Missouri line. Quantrill had lost half a dozen men at most, including the drunken Larkin Skaggs, left behind in Lawrence. Once in Missouri, the guerrilla bands broke away and disappeared into the countryside.

Chapter 21

Order No. 11

I t surprised no one that James Lane was the first to use the bloodshed
to his advantage," wrote historian Ronald D. Smith of the Lawrence
Massacre. "Lane telegraphed Lincoln that Kansas would have their revenge
on Missouri even if Kansans had to fire on Union forces."[207] The news came
as the besieged Union was beginning to enjoy the victories of Gettysburg
and Vicksburg. The tide was turning, and here was this piece of news. What
was wrong with Kansas?

As Quantrill's raiders left Lawrence, Lane (still in his nightshirt) rallied
anyone to be had and anything to be ridden in pursuit of the band. The
effect was far more for show, but in fairness to Lane, the only other option
would have been to do nothing. He gathered the resources left to him in the
ashes of Lawrence.

The man charged with protecting Kansas was General Thomas Ewing
Jr., Charles Robinson's friend, though Robinson was no longer governor.
Terms only lasted two years at that time, so Thomas Carney was the chief
executive. The three jockeyed for power, but as long as Lane was in the good
graces of Lincoln, he would win.

Lane summoned Ewing to meet him on the border, just inside Cass
County, Missouri. The conversation between Ewing and Lane after the raid
was not pretty. Ewing had pursued Quantrill, too, with Ohio troops who
happened to be at Fort Leavenworth. The federals were just too far behind.
Some of his soldiers had died from heatstroke. Many of the men killed in the
massacre had been friends of Ewing's for years. Lane was not the only one

who keenly felt this loss, but Lane unleashed his fury on Ewing. He screamed at the general:

> *Mincing no words, Lane accused the general of following a milk-and-water policy along the border. "Unless you do something and do it fast," he threatened, "to clean out Quantrill and his murdering thieves, you will be a dead dog, Ewing!"*[208]

Though not all historians agree, this is Castel's account of what happened next:

> *Ewing detested Lane personally. But Lane was the king of Kansas politics, and Ewing had political ambitions. Therefore, he sought to appease the irate Senator. Taking him aside to a log cabin, he wrote out in his presence the rough draft of a military proclamation which, he vowed, would take care of the bushwhackers once and for all. Lane read it, said this was more like it, and promised not to make trouble for Ewing.*[209]

Perhaps Lane envisioned the impact of the action they were discussing; it is difficult to imagine that anyone would have understood the true result and still have supported it.

On August 25, 1863, while the residents of Lawrence were still burying their dead, General Ewing issued General Order No. 11, one of the most draconian actions the United States government ever perpetrated against its own citizens. In order to create a demilitarized zone, an area just inside the border where it would no longer be possible to harbor guerrillas, the order called for every citizen in the countryside of Jackson, Cass and Bates Counties and part of Vernon County, Missouri, to vacate within fifteen days. While there was a legitimate military objective, the order was also punitive.

George Caleb Bingham, the noted artist, was an influential and wealthy man. He had leased property in Kansas City to the Union army. Weeks earlier, another controversial order had been issued that involved Bingham, though indirectly. Several women related to the bushwhackers were jailed in the end unit of row houses belonging to Bingham. These women had not committed any crime, but since Missouri was under martial law, that didn't really matter. They were related to men believed to be key in Confederate guerrilla operations—that was crime enough.

Several soldiers were occupying the adjacent building as guards. They often pulled wood from the prison unit for firewood, to the point that the building became unstable. Officials ignored reports that it was unsafe, and on August 13, days before the raid on Lawrence, the building collapsed. Five women were killed, including Josephine Anderson, the sister of guerrilla Bill Anderson. Another sister was crippled. Bill's youngest sister, age ten, was a prisoner as well.

The jail collapse sent Bill Anderson over the edge. Whatever he had been before the death of his sister, afterward he was a monomaniacal killing machine. He vowed to kill as many Yankees as possible, wearing his notable silk cord with a knot for each of them he personally killed.

Bingham, though a Unionist, thought that Order No. 11 was going too far. Perhaps he felt guilty by association since he owned the building in which the girls had died. Personally witnessing the atrocities that took place after the

Confederate guerrilla William "Bloody Bill" Anderson after he was killed near Orrick, Missouri, in 1864. During Quantrill's Raid on Lawrence, Anderson was said to have killed fourteen men. He wore a silk cord with a knot for every Yankee he personally dispatched. At his death, the cord had fifty-four knots. It is included in a collection at the Museum of World Treasures in Wichita, Kansas. Considered macabre today, death photos were common in the nineteenth and early twentieth centuries. Images of famous people, especially outlaws who had been killed, were sold as postcards. *Kansas State Historical Society.*

order was enacted, he painted the scene with Ewing as the focal point. It is another irony that a Unionist preserved one of the most damning moments in the exercise of federal authority over those considered in rebellion.

Years later, Missourian Mrs. Frances Twyman recalled the effect of the war on her family:

Our homes were invaded and ransacked by the Federal soldiers and women and children were dragged off to prison. Not content with all of this, Tom Ewing issued that terrible Order No. 11. I try to forgive, but I cannot—no, cannot—forget. If Tom Ewing is in heaven today his inner life must have greatly changed. Never can I forget the many scenes of misery and distress I saw on the road when people were ordered to leave their homes on a few days' notice. The road from Independence to Lexington was crowded with women and children, women walking with their babies in their arms, packs on their backs, and four or five children following after them—some crying for bread, some crying to be taken back to their homes. Alas! They knew not that their once happy homes were gone. The torch had been applied—nothing left to tell the tale of carnage but the chimneys. O, how sad! I saw one woman driving an ox team (the soldiers had taken nearly all the horses); there were three or four small children in the wagon. We came to a bridge that was almost perpendicular (the teams had to be taken out and the wagons taken down by hand); the oxen scented water, and she lost control of them; so here they went helter-skelter down the bridge. It looked like the wagon would turn a somersault over the oxen. We all thought the children would be killed, but a kind Providence watched over them. I will never forget how the mother looked, as she stood there helpless, crying and wringing her hands as she gave vent to her feelings by saying, "I wish all the Federals were in ___."

...I was arrested several times, came near being shot twice and our horses were taken from us. But alas! Our worst troubles were yet to come. Our daughter Julia, just budding into womanhood, was taken sick and died...The hardships we had to endure under Order No. 11 were too much for one of her delicate nature. She was my only daughter. She was too pure for this earth. God took my darling Julia to dwell with Him.

The home of my mother, 72 years old, was burned. She had neither husband or son. She was an invalid, confined to her bed. She was accused of sending a ham of meat to Quantrill's camp. It was a false accusation, but she owned slaves and had to suffer for it although innocent of the charge against her.[210]

Volumes can be written on the heartbreak that resulted from Order No. 11. It was like spreading the Lawrence Massacre literally over western Missouri. The incursions back and forth over the border during the territorial period had escalated into unspeakable and widespread horror. Devastated emotionally and materially, citizens of both states had to wonder if it would ever end.

Chapter 22

Mine Creek

On October 8, 1864, Kansas governor Thomas Carney called out the state militia with the same "restrained" rhetoric that had defined the border war:

> *The State is in peril! Price and his rebel hosts threaten it with invasion…*
> *Men of Kansas, rally! One blow, one earnest, united blow, will foil the invader and save you. Who will falter? Who is not ready to meet the peril? Who will not defend his home and the State?*
> *To arms, then! To arms and the tented field, until the rebel foe shall be baffled and beaten back.*[211]

Again? General Sterling Price would reclaim Missouri. It must have been torturous for the former governor to witness the bloodshed and chaos that had wracked his state. Most of Price's officers were also Missourians, and they wanted to take back their home. The plan was bold: Price and his men would come out of Arkansas and would sweep through Missouri, picking up troops and supplies as they went. Missouri would welcome them with open arms, and there would be enough new recruits to repel any of the Union advances that might be mounted. Traveling with Price was the exiled Confederate governor Thomas C. Reynolds. Upon reaching Jefferson City, the Union government would be captured and the Confederate government installed. It was almost reminiscent of the competing governments of Bleeding Kansas. Since this was an election year, losing Missouri would be a blow to Lincoln's reelection. That could turn the tide of the war for the Confederacy. From there, Price would turn his attention to Kansas, specifically Fort Leavenworth, with its storehouses of weapons and ammunition.

"After a successful capture of Fort Leavenworth, Price was to turn south and journey through eastern Kansas capturing what he could and destroying all that stood in his way," wrote historian Jeffrey D. Stalnaker.[212]

General Price, hero of the Mexican-American War and a former congressman, was a larger-than-life figure, in achievement and stature. At six feet, six inches tall and more than three hundred pounds, he was so large that he rode a carriage instead of a horse most of the time—not a commanding position for a general. He did bring along a huge white steed that he mounted for special occasions or for dramatic effect. With Price were Generals Joseph O. Shelby and John S. Marmaduke, as well as General James Fagan with troops from Arkansas.

As the army of twelve thousand cavalry (actually, mostly mounted infantry) made its way through Missouri, it gathered wagons of supplies and became slower and more cumbersome—it had to be protected.

Major General Samuel Curtis, commanding the Department of Kansas with headquarters at Fort Leavenworth, had a mere four thousand soldiers to protect the far-flung settlements along the Santa Fe and California Trails

The Kansas Militia was called into service to repel General Sterling Price during his invasion of Missouri. The Battle of the Blue was one of the actions along Price's route, followed by the Battles of Westport and Mine Creek. *Kansas State Historical Society.*

from Indian attacks in one part of his district, as well as to protect Unionists from rebels in the remainder. It was nearly impossible to do either with the resources at his disposal. When he received word that Price was coming back with an army, he called Major General Blunt back from western Kansas and wired Governor Carney informing him that he needed Kansas militia to help repel this invasion. The governor was slow in responding.

As the army moved north, military commanders all over Missouri prepared to meet the assault. General William Rosecrans commanded the Department of Missouri, with headquarters in St. Louis. He knew that Price could only come into the state by one of three routes: into southeastern Missouri via Pocahontas, north toward Jefferson City by West Plains and Rolla or north to the Missouri River by way of Springfield (or the Kansas border). He concentrated regular units at St. Louis.[213]

When General Price learned that General Rosecrans had reinforced St. Louis, he shifted his destination to Pilot Knob, a fortification some fifty miles south of the city. On September 27, who should slow Price's progress but General Thomas Ewing, who had been moved from Kansas during the aftermath of Quantrill's raid and Order No. 11.

At Pilot Knob, Missouri, Ewing's forces of only one thousand men managed to hold off the assault of Marmaduke's and Fagan's divisions. The Confederate casualties were more than the total number of men Ewing commanded. Ewing had two hundred men killed, wounded or missing and knew that he could not take a second assault. In a remarkable maneuver, Ewing managed to sneak his men out of the fort under the cover of darkness. When Fagan and Marmaduke prepared to battle the next morning, there was no enemy to fight.

General Ewing had gained valuable intelligence on the strength and location of Price's army while inflicting heavy casualties and saving his own command in the process. Swinging westward, General Price arrived in Boonville, where as many as 1,500 men joined his forces. Here he met with Bloody Bill Anderson, the guerrilla leader who greatly admired Price and presented him a gift of a set of pistols. Price wanted to make the most of the bushwhacker's talents and sent him to sabotage the North Missouri Railroad. (This would result in one of the most heinous acts of the war, one that Price would never have sanctioned: the Centralia Massacre.)

The longer this invasion dragged out, the closer it came to election day. Governor Carney wanted to give Kansas soldiers time to vote before sending them to battle. More than sixteen thousand men in militia units answered the governor's call—enough to win a battle or an election but not both, feared Carney.[214]

As Price's army and entourage lumbered toward Kansas, it was moving so slowly that people began to think that his army had turned to the south and that the danger had passed. When Union forces under General James Blunt skirmished with General Jo Shelby's men at Lexington, Kansas knew that this was not a false alarm. Shelby followed Blunt to the Little Blue River. There was an issue, however, about just how far outside Kansas militia units could serve, and Blunt was ordered to make this a delaying action rather than a battle, thereby bringing the Missourians close enough to Kansas to legitimize their participation.[215]

After several hours of fighting, the Federals marched through Independence, about nine miles away, and retreated to the Big Blue, while Price's army camped at Independence. The next day, Price easily broke the Union lines. When the day ended, a Confederate victory was within Price's grasp. But when Union general Alfred Pleasanton finally arrived and attacked Marmaduke at Price's rear, it changed the course of events. The next day found the Confederates nearly surrounded, and Shelby fought long enough to allow Price and that incredible wagon train to escape to the south.

Guilford Gage was a private defending Kansas in the Battle of the Blue. Later, as a successful businessman, he memorialized the sacrifices of his comrades by moving the remains of those buried on the battlefield to Topeka Cemetery and erecting an elaborate monument to the bravery of the men from Topeka who fought. *Kansas State Historical Society.*

"All along the way, broken wagons, blankets, arms boxes, tack, trash, rifles and anything undesirable to the rank and file Rebel soldier was tossed aside," wrote Jeffrey D. Stalnaker. "The wagon train stretched for miles and was extremely slow."[216]

Union pursuers were not far behind Price's army. Near Trading Post, some settlers had been murdered, likely by some of Jo Shelby's Missourians. The ever-eloquent apologist Major John Newman Edwards wrote that "Shelby was soothing the wounds of Missouri by stabbing the breast of Kansas."[217]

Price retreated until he reached Mine Creek in southeastern Kansas, north of Fort Scott, where his wagons became mired in the creek crossing. The ensuing battle was the second-largest cavalry clash of the Civil War, with a combined cavalry of twelve thousand. (Brandy Station, Virginia, in June 1863 was the largest, with twenty thousand total cavalry. Union general Alfred Pleasanton had been the commander in that battle, with Confederate forces led by General J.E.B. Stuart).

One of the Union officers, Colonel Samuel Crawford, who was to protect Fort Scott, recalled of Mine Creek:

Mine Creek was one of the most important of all the battles ever fought on the soil of Kansas. General Price with an army of about nine thousand

Samuel Crawford was attached to the staff of General Curtis during the invasion of Missouri by Sterling Price. A colonel at the time, he was elected to the governorship of Kansas during the war and was a brevet general in the spring of 1865. He was reelected but resigned during his second term of office to command a regiment for service in the Plains Indian Wars. *Kansas State Historical Society.*

ragged, hungry soldiers, after a wild reckless raid through Missouri, was trying to make his escape through Kansas and back to the dismal swamps of the Sunny South. He had been fighting and running for thirty consecutive days and his deluded followers were crying for bread.[218]

Crawford's comments about the condition of the Confederate soldiers were true and more. The soldiers fit the stereotypical end-of-war rebel: ragged, hungry, poorly armed and proud.

The Union forces prepared to attack, fully expecting the Confederates to crumble at the sight of this overwhelming cavalry charge. Historian Edgar Langsdorf noted:

The order to charge was given, Benteen against Price's right and Phillips against his center and left. The Tenth Missouri started forward, bugles sounding, but they hesitated and came to a stop half way down the slope when the enemy showed no sign of breaking. In spite of repeated commands from Benteen and other officers they did not resume the charge, apparently brought up short by some strange psychological block. There was danger that the regiments following them would be thrown into confusion.[219]

Historian Jeffrey Stalnaker added:

The Rebel troopers, sitting bravely in their saddles, stood static in their defensive positions, stiffened and waiting for the first horse to crash into their lines with a determination to stand their ground. The advance ground to a halt. The Tenth Missouri had inexplicably and suddenly halted. The men and horses of the Fourth Iowa, the Third Iowa and the consolidated Seventh Indiana/Fourth Missouri were stacking up behind the Tenth until it became one mass of horse and man turning about.[220]

As Benteen was screaming, begging, urging his men to move, the major commanding the Fourth Iowa took the initiative and attacked to the left. "This movement seemed to break the spell of the [regiment] and the Tenth regained its poise and followed," wrote Langsdorf. "They struck the enemy line from left to right, broke it, and 'it all fell away like a row of bricks.'" The fighting, though brief, impressed Benteen as surpassing any he had ever seen.[221]

The Sharps carbine won the day. Armed with muzzleloaders and unable to fire as quickly from their mounts as the Union cavalrymen, the Confederates wheeled their horses to retreat, and as they left the field, they broke their own defensive lines in the rear. General Price tried to rally his troops. Mounting his white charger, he shouted encouragement to his routed men.

The Confederate forces could not stand up to a force that was "better armed, better trained and more motivated."[222] The motivation was ridding Kansas of the rebel threat for good. General Marmaduke was among the nine hundred Confederate prisoners, and the Iowa private who captured him was awarded the Congressional Medal of Honor.

One of the most controversial aspects of the Battle at Mine Creek was the execution of Confederate prisoners wearing blue overcoats. Part of the captured cargo in those cumbersome wagons were Union coats. With autumn closing in, nighttime temperatures were cold. The coats were distributed among the men. The letter of the law stated that anyone wearing the uniform of his enemy would be considered a spy and subject to execution.

General Price's campaign failed on so many levels; far from taking Missouri for the Confederacy, the Union hold on the state was solidified. Much of the plunder the soldiers had taken was forfeited at Mine Creek, either destroyed or confiscated by the Yankees. The Federals pursued Price's army back into Arkansas but did not catch it. As with most events in Kansas, in the end it was all about Jim Lane.

Most of the Kansas militiamen were home for election day of 1864. Colonel Crawford was elected governor of Kansas, with his term set to begin on January 9, 1865. President Lincoln was reelected, in part due to the actions of Jim Lane at the nominating convention earlier that year. The election results overall were a testament to Lane's political sway over the Republican Party in Kansas. As Bryce Benedict commented, "Kansas had become a two-party state—Lane, and anti-Lane."[223] Most of this can be attributed to his relationship with President Lincoln, but Albert Castel pointed out that part of the reason the anti-Lane folks were defeated was their mishandling of Price's invasion:

> [Governor] *Carney's unwillingness to call out the military, the foolish statements of the Times…And other Carney adherents that Price was not in Missouri, the mutinies and desertions in the militia traceable to the statements, and Carney's intention to disband the militia with Price only a*

Mary Lane divorced her controversial husband, James H Lane, once but later remarried him. *Kansas State Historical Society.*

few miles from the state, all combined to make the Governor and his faction appear not only unpatriotic but fatuous. The Lane newspapers did not fail to make the most of these errors by "Carney and his bolting copperhead crew" and to contrast them unfavorably with the supposedly heroic exploits of Lane and Crawford in repelling Price and saving Kansas.[224]

Paraphrasing the Bible, all things worked together for Lane.

Epilogue

The elections of the autumn of 1864 had virtually ensured that Jim Lane would be reelected to the U.S. Senate. The Lane Republicans would control the Kansas legislature and would send their patron back to Washington. Lane was understandably quite relieved.

Despite the border conflicts during the Civil War itself, Kansas managed to grow and prosper. When word of the Confederate surrender came in April 1865, Kansans looked forward to realizing all the dreams they had put on hold throughout the war. In the Northern states, people were hopeful for the first time in years. At this celebratory moment, President Abraham Lincoln was assassinated. The nation reeled.

Perhaps only Mary Lincoln's grief was more severe than that of Senator James Lane. With the death of Lincoln, Lane's benefactor was gone. The anti-Lane folks in Kansas could not have been happy at the news of Lincoln's death, but the second thought that occurred to them had to be that, at last, Jim Lane's power would be gone.

Upon the president's death, Vice President Andrew Johnson became the nation's chief executive at what might have been the second most difficult time in the nation's history. Possessing neither Lincoln's ability as a politician nor his vision, Johnson faced the task of what to do with the South. Johnson endeavored to carry out the policies of Lincoln, "let 'em up easy." Radical Republicans, however, saw harsher penalties for Southern traitors and fought Johnson tooth and nail. Lane, hoping to ingratiate himself to Johnson as he had Lincoln, promised to support Johnson's efforts in return for the continued ability to make political appointments back in Kansas. With Lincoln out of the picture, however, the Radicals were unleashed on Lane. Stories of corruption began to appear in the press. Lane had survived assaults on his character before, but he would not survive this one. He suffered a mental collapse. On July 1, 1866, Jim Lane put a pistol in his mouth and pulled the trigger. He lingered for ten days. It is often said that there is symbolism in the method of suicide one chooses. That Lane chose a gun is significant, of course, for its suddenness and dramatic effect. That he placed a gun in his mouth must have been significant, too. The words that had come from that mouth had confounded and commanded, infuriated and inspired. All those words were now gone.

Appointed to fill Lane's Senate seat was Edmund G. Ross, a bright and ambitious businessman from Topeka, who was aligned with the Radicals of his party until he reached Washington and the weight of his office settled on his shoulders.

Impeachment proceedings were brought against President Johnson, and Ross's supporters made it very clear how he was to vote. Despite a personal dislike of Johnson, Ross found no legal reason to remove him from office. Kansans were livid. The political career of E.G. Ross was over as far as Kansas was concerned.

Edmund G. Ross was a publisher and businessman in Topeka. He served in the Eleventh Kansas Infantry, first as captain and later as major. He and his men went to aid Lawrence following the massacre in 1863. In 1866, Governor Samuel Crawford appointed him to fill the vacancy in the Senate created by the suicide of James H. Lane. *Kansas State Historical Society.*

One of the most poignant testaments to Ross's sacrifice is found in Topeka Cemetery. The E.G. Ross plot is located near the center of the graveyard, a prime spot. Visitors walk past it without so much as a glance because the plot is empty save for the small, flat marker of four-year-old Flynt Ross. Kansas was Ross's home; he and his brothers had come with high ideals and notions of making fortunes. He had planned someday to rest peacefully beside his child, but he knowingly risked all to vote his conscience.

With the threat of Southern invasion gone, Kansas was as close to peace as it had been since the territory was opened for settlement. But joy was always tempered by the memory of the incredible losses. Many of those early settlers who had come to Kansas with such high hopes had not survived. Some returned to their homes in the East, and others sought fortune in the West.

Many who had passed through Kansas had gone on to achieve acclaim during the war, on one side or the other. Colonel E.V. Sumner became a general in the Union army; his adjutant, Lieutenant J.E.B. Stuart, became a general in the Confederate army. Neither survived the war. General Sumner died at his home in New York, just before he was to return to the west to take command of his old stomping grounds. On March 29, 1863, the *New York Times* reported on the officer's death:

> *The dying soldier attempted vainly to speak intelligibly to those about him. At last, when a glass of wine was handed him, he took it in his hand, and with a great effort waved it above his head, and spoke in a voice as clear as ever, "God save my country, the United States of America." These were the last words of the patriot hero.*

William Clarke Quantrill died shortly after the war ended; mortally wounded by counter-guerrillas in Kentucky, he lingered for one month in a Louisville hospital. Until recently, he did not rest in peace, as his bones were collected by souvenir hunters in Ohio and by historians in Kansas. He is now buried in the Confederate Cemetery at Higginsville, Missouri.

William T. Sherman, who may have reached the low point of his life as a lawyer and speculator in the Kansas Territory, became a Union general and devastated the South, much as his foster brother and brother-in-law, Thomas Ewing Jr., had devastated western Missouri. Interesting family to be sure.

General Edwin Sumner was being reassigned to the West when he took ill and died at his home in Syracuse, New York, in 1863. *Author's collection.*

Young Willie Cody enlisted in the Seventh Kansas Cavalry in February 1864 at the age of eighteen. He recalled that he was drunk when he enlisted, and while he had the thirst for adventure, he really could not stomach Jayhawking. His later service in the army in the West was invaluable, and he was awarded the Medal of Honor. As Buffalo Bill Cody, he took the story of Kansas and the American West to the world.

The transplanted Pennsylvanian Cyrus K. Holliday realized his dreams of seeing Topeka become the state capital and of building a railroad. As founder of the Atchison, Topeka and Santa Fe Railroad, Holliday enjoyed a successful career and the respect of his neighbors.

Ten years after he had fled Kansas, the former territorial governor Andrew Reeder returned to Tecumseh and finished his chess game with Julia Stinson. Julia won.

Over the course of its tumultuous territorial days, ten men would serve as governor or acting governor. Daniel Woodson and Hugh Walsh were acting governor four times each. Walsh stayed in Kansas and wanted the job but apparently did not have the clout to get the appointment. Fry Giles wrote of the situation:

> *It is a most singular political mystery, that no one of the six men successively appointed by Presidents Pierce and Buchanan to be Governors of Kansas should have known the political work they were expected to do. It is reasonable to assume that they did not. They were all eminent in the national councils of the Democratic party; they all became acceptable to the Free-State party soon after their arrival upon the field; they were all removed or forced to resign within a few months from the date of their appointment (with the exception of Gov. Medary), and for no alleged cause.*[225]

In fairness, no one could have prepared these men for the unique situation they found in Kansas. There were so many unknowns and so many competing elements. The world around them was changing more and more quickly as they were swept along by the tide of history.

During the Civil War, soldiers served Kansas throughout the conflict in places far from the volatile border. These men were not native Kansans; they had come west to make new homes and new lives and sacrificed all in service to their adopted home and their nation. Kansas had a disproportionately high number of soldiers enlisted in comparison to the overall population. That remains true today. Kansas continues to exert a disproportionate impact on the military in other ways, especially through the Army's Command and General Staff College at Fort Leavenworth, "the intellectual center of the army." Modern leaders such as Generals Frederick Funston, Dwight D. Eisenhower and Richard Myers demonstrate that the world still looks to Kansas for leadership.

John Steuart Curry chose well when he selected the elements of the statehouse mural, with John Brown at the center, not only because Brown so dominated early Kansas but also because he expresses the commitment and passion of Kansans for a cause. Perhaps the most interesting image is not Brown but rather what is happening behind him—the wagons have not stopped because of the warfare.

Despite the difficulties, Kansans continue to look to the stars with their feet planted firmly in this rich soil.

Appendix

Following the Civil War, so many veterans moved to Kansas that it was nicknamed the "Soldier State." The roll call of county and town names is an honor roll of the war: Geary, Sedgwick, Scott, McPherson, Reno, Grant, Kearny, Sherman, Logan, Sheridan, Leavenworth, Thomas, Meade, Wallace, Rice, Crawford, Lyon and Barton (for Civil War nurse Clara Barton, the only woman for whom a Kansas county is named). These were names known throughout the nation. Many of these people were honored by the troops who knew them and served with them. But what of the lesser-known men for whom Kansas counties are named?

Ellis County honors George Ellis, first lieutenant, Company I, Twelfth Kansas Infantry, killed in battle on April 30, 1864, at Jenkin's Ferry, Arkansas.

Harper County is named for Marion Harper, first sergeant, Company E, Second Regiment, Kansas Cavalry, who was mortally wounded at Waldron, Arkansas, on December 29, 1863. He died the following day.

Hodgeman County is named in memory of Captain Amos Hodgman, Company H, Seventh Kansas Cavalry. He was wounded in action on October 10, 1863, at Wyatt, Mississippi, and died six days later. The county honoring him misspelled his name.

Jewell County is named for Lieutenant Lewis R. Jewell, Sixth Kansas Cavalry, who was mortally wounded at Cane Hill, Arkansas, and died on November 30, 1862.

Mitchell County honors William D. Mitchell, who was a private in Company K, Second Kansas Cavalry, but moved to the Second Kentucky

John M. Whitehead served in the Fifteenth Indiana Infantry as a chaplain, earning the nickname "the bloody chaplain" because he attended to wounded soldiers on the battlefield and constantly became covered in their blood. He was awarded the Congressional Medal of Honor for his service to his fellow soldiers. Among the thousands of soldiers who made Kansas their home following the war, he moved to Topeka and helped establish the First Baptist Church. He is interred at Topeka Cemetery. *Author's collection.*

Cavalry and was promoted to captain. He died at Monroe's Crossroads, North Carolina, on March 10, 1865, just a month before the war ended.

Ness County honors Corporal Noah Ness, Company G, Seventh Kansas Cavalry. Ness died on August 22, 1864, at Abbyville, Mississippi, having been wounded in battle three days earlier.

Pratt County memorializes Caleb Pratt, second lieutenant, Company D, First Kansas Infantry, killed during the battle at Wilson's Creek, Missouri, on August 10, 1861.

Rooks County was named for Private John C. Rooks, Company I, Eleventh Kansas Infantry. He was wounded at the Battle of Prairie Grove on December 7, 1862, and died four days later.

Russell County honors another young man who fought at Prairie Grove, Captain Alva P. Russell, Company K, Second Kansas Cavalry, who died on December 12, 1862.

The monument to Kansas soldiers at the Chattanooga Battlefield. Author's collection.

Smith County was named for Major Nathan Smith, Second Colorado Volunteers, killed on October 23, 1864, at the Little Blue in Missouri repelling the invasion of General Sterling Price.

Trego County was named for Captain Edgar P. Trego, Company H, Eighth Kansas Infantry, who was killed at Chickamauga, Georgia, on September 19, 1863.

Other counties, like Barber and Phillips, were named for martyrs to the free state cause. And, of course, there is Lincoln County, which honors the commander in chief of the Union forces during the Civil War. Because of the time during which Kansas was settled, it is doubtful that any other state honors so many veterans of the Civil War.

Notes

Introduction

1. Greg Case, a native of Salina, Kansas, is the CEO of Aon in Chicago, Illinois.

Chapter 1

2. Russell, "Julia Cody Goodman's Memoirs," 455.
3. Cody, *Life of Hon. William F. Cody*, 40.
4. Gray, "Fact versus Fiction," 4.
5. Russell, "Julia Cody Goodman's Memoirs," 458–59.
6. Ibid., 459.
7. Cody, *Life of Hon. William F. Cody*, 41.
8. Russell, "Julia Cody Goodman's Memoirs," 459.
9. Cody, *Life of Hon. William F. Cody*, 42.
10. Russell, "Julia Cody Goodman's Memoirs," 460.
11. Gray, "Fact versus Fiction," 5.
12. Russell, "Julia Cody Goodman's Memoirs," 465–66.

Chapter 2

13. Savage, Recollections of 1854, Territorial Kansas Online.
14. Pierse to Eli Thayer, March 31, 1857, Kansas State Historical Society (KSHS).
15. Etcheson, "Great Principle of Self-Government," 17.
16. Isely and Richards, *Story of Kansas*, 50.
17. Etcheson, "Great Principle of Self-Government," 17.
18. Ibid., 43.

Chapter 3

19. Benton, "Discourse of Mr. Benton," 1–3.
20. Ibid., 15.
21. Ibid., 1–2.
22. Giles, *Thirty Years in Topeka*, 51–54. Giles added that Fremont Street became Fillmore in later years, "though by what authority we are not able to state."
23. Holliday to Mary Holliday, December 31, 1854, KSHS.
24. Ibid.
25. Miner, "Historic Ground," 13.
26. Holliday, November 18, 1854, KSHS.
27. Giles, *Thirty Years in Topeka*, 27.
28. Holliday, December 17, 1854, KSHS.
29. Fitzgerald, *John Ritchie*, 14–15.
30. Lindquist, "Letters of the Rev. Samuel," 67.

Chapter 4

31. Brown, to wife, October 13, 1855, KSHS.
32. Brown, to wife, October 13–14, 1855, KSHS.
33. Ibid.
34. Dirck, "By the Hand of God," 106.
35. Ibid., 106–7.
36. Ibid., 106.

Chapter 5

37. Prentis, *History of Kansas*, 45.
38. Isely and Richards, *Story of Kansas*, 52.
39. Stewart diary, online transcription from *Kansas Historical Quarterly*, 1–36.

Chapter 6

40. Hickman, "Reeder Administration Inaugurated," 310.
41. Ibid., 311
42. Savage, Recollections of 1854, Territorial Kansas Online.
43. KSHS, August 1937, 246.
44. Hickman, "Reeder Administration Inaugurated," 312.
45. *Kansas City Star*, February 7, 1915.
46. Hickman, "Reeder Administration Inaugurated," 333–40.

Chapter 7

47. Isely, *Early Days in Kansas*, 54–56.
48. Blackmar, *Kansas*, 855.
49. KSHS.org, Thomas Barber Biography.
50. The Whittier poem appears on two granite grave covers on Barber's plot in the Pioneer Cemetery, Lawrence, Kansas.
51. Blackmar, *Kansas*, 856–57.

Chapter 8

52. *Boston Traveller*, "Letters from Kansas," October 6, 1856.
53. Holliday to Mary Holliday, December 31, 1854, KSHS.
54. Stewart diary, 1–36.
55. Holzer, "Lincoln-Douglas Debates."
56. Wagnon, "Wrecking Slavery from the Kansas Territory," March 4, 2005.
57. Holliday to Mary Holliday, June 16, 1856, KSHS.
58. Rutherford, "*Arabia* Incident," 39–47.

59. Wagnon, "Wrecking Slavery."
60. *Kansas Weekly Herald*, May 10, 1856.
61. Wagnon, "Wrecking Slavery."
62. Brewerton, *Wars of the Western Border*, 270.
63. Ibid., 270–72.
64. Ibid., 272.
65. Ibid., 273.
66. Ibid., 274.
67. Isely, *Early Days in Kansas*, 57–59; Brewerton, *Wars of the Western Border*, 274.
68. Martin, "Mahala Doyle," 31.
69. *Report of the Special Committee to Investigate the Troubles in Kansas.*
70. Ibid.

CHAPTER 9

71. Goodrich, "Dog Day at Blackjack," 13.
72. Scrapbook of clippings in author's collection; this appears to have come from an 1856 newspaper article.
73. Holliday to Mary Holliday, June 17, 1856, KSHS.
74. Senate Executive Documents, 53.
75. Ibid.
76. KSHS biography, online at www.kshs.org/kansapedia/pardee-butler/12000.
77. Wallace, *Capital's Storied Capitols*, 56–57.
78. Ibid., 58.
79. Ibid.
80. Secretary of War Jefferson Davis would later quibble with Sumner on the exact meaning of the orders, as Davis was prone to second-guessing and micromanagement. Sumner, like Davis, was so earnest in his determination to do right that he strongly resented his actions being questioned.

CHAPTER 10

81. Wilder, *Annals of Kansas*, 132.

82. Brown, "Account of the Battle of Osawatomie," online at www. territorialkansasonline.com.
83. Ibid.
84. Wilder, *Annals of Kansas*, 134.
85. Senate Executive Documents, Report of the Secretary of War, 99.
86. Wilder, *Annals of Kansas*, 136.
87. Senate Executive Documents, Report of the Secretary of War, 97–98.
88. Ibid., 98.
89. Ibid., 99.
90. Ibid., 97.

Chapter 11

91. Gray, "Fact versus Fiction," 10.
92. Senate Executive Documents, Report of the Secretary of War, 119–20.
93. Ibid., 84–85.
94. Ibid., 84–85.
95. Martin, "Recollections of Early Times in Kansas Territory," *Transactions of the Kansas State Historical Society*, 496.
96. Ibid.
97. Goodrich, "Somewhere Along the Solomon," 8.
98. Martin, "Recollections of Early Times in Kansas Territory," *Transactions of the Kansas State Historical Society*, 497.
99. Ibid., 499.
100. Ibid.
101. Ibid., 500.
102. Ibid., 505.
103. Ibid., 507.

Chapter 12

104. Dirck, "By the Hand of God," 109.
105. Blackmar, *Kansas*, 303; Dirck, "By the Hand of God," 106.
106. Hougen, "Marias des Cygnes Massacre," 80.
107. Ibid., 83.

108. Ibid.
109. Ibid., 85.
110. Rich, *Heritage of Kansas*, 49.
111. Hougen, 91.
112. Neely, *Border Between Them*, 72.
113. Ibid.
114. Mildfelt, *Secret Danites*, 73; Dirck, "By the Hand of God," 107.
115. Neely, *Border Between Them*, 74; Mildfelt, *Secret Danites*, 73; Dirck, "By the Hand of God," 107.

Chapter 13

116. Martin, "The Battle of the Spurs," *Transactions of the Kansas State Historical Society*, 444.
117. Mildfelt, *Secret Danites*, 74–75.
118. Ibid.
119. Gilmore, *Civil War on the Missouri-Kansas Border*, 98.
120. Wagnon, "Wrecking Slavery."
121. Fitzgerald, *John Ritchie*, 18–31.
122. Martin, "The Battle of the Spurs," *Transactions of the Kansas State Historical Society*, 445.
123. Ibid., 447.
124. Ibid., 448.

Chapter 14

125. Davis, *JEB Stuart*, 10.
126. Rich, *Heritage of Kansas*, 41.
127. Castel, *Frontier State at War*, 23.
128. Martin, "An Attempted Rescue of John Brown From Charlestown, VA., Jail," *Transactions of the Kansas State Historical Society*, 216–17.
129. Ibid., 225.
130. *Report*, 34th Congress, 1st Session, 1,193.
131. John Ritchie to Aaron D. Stevens, March 7, 1860, KSHS.
132. Goodrich, "Biography—John Brown," 9.

133. Smith, *Thomas Ewing Jr.*, 100.

134. Beemer, *Deadliest Woman in the West*, 190–91.

135. Ibid., 191; Territorial Death Records, KSHS.

136. Smith, *Thomas Ewing Jr.*, 109.

137. *Topeka State Record*, April 23, 1860.

138. Ibid.

139. Giles, *Thirty Years in Topeka*, 138–40.

140. Rice, "Reminiscences," handwritten ms transcribed by Bryce Benedict, KSHS; Giles, *Thirty Years in Topeka*, 138–43.

141. *Topeka Tribune*, May 19, 1860.

142. Rice, "Reminiscences."

Chapter 15

143. Waskie, *Philadelphia and the Civil War*, 48.

144. Ibid.

145. Ibid, 49.

146. Castel, *Frontier State at War*, 19–20.

147. Ibid., 19.

148. Ibid.

149. Ibid., 21.

150. Smith, *Thomas Ewing Jr.*, 129.

151. Randall, *Mary Lincoln*, 190.

152. Benedict, *Jayhawkers*, 26–28.

153. Castel, *Frontier State at War*, 35.

154. Smith, *Thomas Ewing Jr.*, 338.

Chapter 16

155. Price, *Nathaniel Lyon*, 1.

156. Ibid., 22.

157. Ibid., 33.

158. Ibid.

159. Castel, *Frontier State at War*, 45.

160. Gilmore, *Civil War on the Missouri-Kansas Border*, 125–26.

161. U.S. War Department, *The War of the Rebellion: A Compilation of the Official Records of the Union and Confederate Armies*, series I, vol. 3, online edition.
162. Ibid.
163. Price, *Nathaniel Lyon*, 56.

CHAPTER 17

164. Castel, *Frontier State at War*, 46.
165. Benedict, *Jayhawkers*, 33.
166. Castel, *Frontier State at War*, 49.
167. Ibid., 51; Gilmore, *Civil War on the Missouri-Kansas Border*, 133.
168. Benedict, *Jayhawkers*, 130–31.
169. Castel, *Frontier State at War*, 55.

CHAPTER 18

170. Benedict, *Jayhawkers*, 257–58.
171. Ibid., 98.
172. Ibid., 103.
173. Ibid.
174. Ibid., 132; Castel, *Frontier State at War*, 63.
175. Gilmore, *Civil War on the Missouri-Kansas Border*, 149.

CHAPTER 19

176. Gilmore, *Civil War on the Missouri-Kansas Border*, 167.
177. Martin, "Quantrill and the Morgan Walker Tragedy," *Transactions of the Kansas State Historical Society*, 324–31.
178. Castel, *William Clarke Quantrill*, 65.
179. Ibid., 65.
180. Gilmore, *Civil War on the Missouri-Kansas Border*, 180.
181. Castel, *William Clarke Quantrill*, 66.
182. Gilmore, *Civil War on the Missouri-Kansas Border*, 180.
183. Castel, *William Clarke Quantrill*, 71.

184. Ibid., 72.

185. Ibid., 73.

186. Ibid., 87–88.

187. Ibid., 95.

188. Gilmore, *Civil War on the Missouri-Kansas Border*, 185–86.

189. Castel, *William Clarke Quantrill*, 95.

190. Gilmore, *Civil War on the Missouri-Kansas Border*, 204; Castel, *William Clarke Quantrill*, 96.

Chapter 20

191. Castel, *William Clarke Quantrill*, 122.

192. Ibid., 122–23; Gilmore, *Civil War on the Missouri-Kansas Border*, 233.

193. Younger, *Story of Cole Younger*, 44–45.

194. Gilmore, *Civil War on the Missouri-Kansas Border*, 236.

195. Castel, *William Clarke Quantrill*, 125.

196. Gilmore, *Civil War on the Missouri-Kansas Border*, 237.

197. Castel, *William Clarke Quantrill*, 126.

198. Peterson, "Letters of Edward and Sarah Fitch," 94.

199. Goodrich, *Black Flag*, 78–79.

200. Gilmore, *Civil War on the Missouri-Kansas Border*, 238.

201. Prentis, *History of Kansas*, 107.

202. Peterson, "Letters of Edward and Sarah Fitch," 95–97.

203. According to Cole Younger's 1903 autobiography, a "negro woman leaned out of a window and shouted: 'You ___ of ___.' She toppled out dead before it was seen she was a woman," 45.

204. For more information on the raid, read Thomas Goodrich's *Bloody Dawn* and see the documentary by the same name produced by Lone Chimney Films.

205. Interview with Greg Hildreth by author, January 2012.

206. Castel, *William Clarke Quantrill*, 129.

Chapter 21

207. Smith, *Thomas Ewing Jr.*, 199.

208. Castel, *William Clarke Quantrill*, 144.
209. Ibid.
210. Chiles, *Tears and Turmoil*, 96–100.

CHAPTER 22

211. Langsdorf and Richard, "Letters of Daniel R. Anthony," 286.
212. Stalnaker, *Battle of Mine Creek*, 32.
213. Langsdorf and Richard, "Letters of Daniel R. Anthony," 284–85.
214. Prentis, *History of Kansas*, 113.
215. Castel, *Frontier State at War*, 192.
216. Stalnaker, *Battle of Mine Creek*, 56.
217. Castel, *Frontier State at War*, 196.
218. Rich, *Heritage of Kansas*, 68.
219. Langsdorf and Richard, "Letters of Daniel R. Anthony," 296.
220. Stalnaker, *Battle of Mine Creek*, 84.
221. Ibid.
222. Ibid., 92.
223. Benedict, *Jayhawkers*, 258.
224. Castel, *Frontier State at War*, 200–201.

EPILOGUE

225. Giles, *Thirty Years in Topeka*, 139.

Bibliography

Beemer, Rod. *The Deadliest Woman in the West: Mother Nature on the Prairies and Plains 1800–1900*. Caldwell, ID: Caxton, 2006.

Benedict, Bryce. *Jayhawkers: The Civil War Brigade of James Henry Lane*. Norman: University of Oklahoma Press, 2009.

Benton, Thomas Hart. "Discourse of Mr. Benton, of Missouri: before the Maryland Institute." Speech delivered on December 5, 1854. Transcription at www.kansasmemory.org.

Billington, Ray Allen. *Westward Expansion: A History of the American Frontier*. New York: McMillan Company, 1949.

Blackmar, Frank W. *Kansas*. Vol. 2. Chicago: Standard Publishing Company, 1912.

Brewerton, Douglas G. *Wars of the Western Border*. New York: Derby and Jackson, 1859.

Castel, Albert. *A Frontier State at War: Kansas, 1861–1865*. Westport, CT: Greenwood Press Inc., 1979. First published by Cornell University Press, 1958.

———. *William Clarke Quantrill: His Life and Times*. 2nd ed. Norman: University of Oklahoma Press, 1999.

Cheatham, Gary L. "'Desperate Characters:' The Development and Impact of the Confederate Guerrillas in Kansas." *Kansas History* 14 (Autumn 1991): 144.

Chiles, Joanne Eakin. *Tears and Turmoil: Order No. 11*. Independence, MO: self-published, 1996.

Clark, Shelley Hickman, and James W. Clark. "Lawrence in 1854: Recollections of Joseph Savage." *Kansas History* 27 (Spring–Summer 2004): 30.

Cody, William F. *The Life of Hon. William F. Cody Known as Buffalo Bill*. Lincoln: University of Nebraska Press, 1978.

Courtwright, Julie. "'A Goblin That Drives Her Insane': Sara Robinson and the History Wars of Kansas, 1894-1911." *Kansas History* 25 (Summer 2002): 102.

Cunningham, Roger D. "Welcoming 'Pa' on the Kaw." *Kansas History* 25 (Summer 2002): 86.

Davis, Burke. *JEB Stuart: The Last Cavalier*. Short Hills, NJ: Burford Books, 1957.

Dirck, Brian R. "By the Hand of God: James Montgomery and Redemptive Violence." *Kansas History* 27 (Spring–Summer 2004): 100.

Etcheson, Nicole. "The Great Principle of Self-Government: Popular Sovereignty and Bleeding Kansas." *Kansas History* 27 (Spring–Summer 2004): 14.

Fisher, Mike. "The First Kansas Colored-Massacreat Poison Springs." *Kansas History* 2 (Summer 1979): 121.

Fitzgerald, Danicl, cd. *John Ritchie: Portrait of an Uncommon Man.* Topeka, KS: Shawnee County Historical Society, November 1991.

Giles, F.W. *Thirty Years in Topeka.* Topeka, KS: Geo. W. Crane and Company Publishers, 1886.

Gilmore, Donald. L. *Civil War on the Missouri-Kansas Border.* Gretna, LA: Pelican Publishing Company, 2006.

Goodrich (Bisel), Debra. "Somewhere Along the Solomon." *Kansas Journal of Military History* 1 (Summer 2005): 8.

Goodrich, Thomas. "Biography—John Brown." *Kansas Journal of Military History* 1 (Spring 2005): 8–10.

———. *Black Flag: Guerrilla Warfare on the Western Border, 1861–1865.* Bloomington: Indiana University Press, 1999.

———. "Dog Day at Blackjack." *Kansas Journal of Military History* 1 (Spring 2005): 12.

Gray, John S. "Fact versus Fiction in the Kansas Boyhood of Buffalo Bill." *Kansas History* 8 (Spring 1985): 2–20.

Gridley, Karl, ed. "'An Idea of Things in Kansas': John Brown's 1857 New England Speech." *Kansas History* 27 (Spring–Summer 2004): 76.

Hart, Charles Desmond. "The Natural Limits of Slavery Expansion: Kansas-Nebraska, 1854." *Kansas Historical Quarterly* 34 (Spring 1968): 32.

Heller, Charles. "George Luther Stearns." *Kansas Journal of Military History* 1 (Spring 2005): 14.

Hickman, Russell K. "The Reeder Administration Inaugurated." *Kansas Historical Quarterly* 36 (Autumn 1970): 305.

Holzer, Harold. "The Lincoln-Douglas Debates Weren't as Great as Gingrich Thinks." *Washington Post,* January 27, 2012.

Hougen, Harvey R. "The Marais des Cygnes Massacre and the Execution of William Griffith." *Kansas History* 8 (Summer 1985): 74–94.

Houts, Joseph K., Jr. *Quantrill's Thieves.* Kansas City, MO: Truman Publishing Company, 2002.

Isely, Bliss. *Early Days in Kansas.* 8th ed. Topeka: Kansas State Teachers Association, 1956.

Isely, Bliss, and W.M. Richards. *The Story of Kansas.* Topeka: Kansas State Board of Education, 1953.

Kansas Historical Quarterly 16. "Letters of Julia Louisa Lovejoy, 1856–1864, Part Four, 1859" (February 1948): 40.

———. "Letters of Julia Louisa Lovejoy, 1856–1864, Part Five, 1860–1864—Concluded" (May 1948): 175.

Kansas State Historical Society, ed. *The Old Pawnee Capitol.* Topeka, KS: self-published, 1928.

Lambert, Don. "The Art of History." *Kansas Journal of Military History* 1 (Spring 2005): 28.

Langsdorf, Edgar, and R.W. Richard. "Letters of Daniel R. Anthony 1857–1862, Part One, 1857." *Kansas Historical Quarterly* 24 (Spring 1958): 6–30.

Lindquist, Emory, ed. "The Letters of the Rev. Samual Young Lum, 'Pioneer Kansas Missionary' 1854–1858, Part One, 1854–1858." *Kansas Historical Quarterly* 25 (Spring 1959): 39.

Martin, George, ed. *Transactions of the Kansas State Historical Society, 1903–1904; Together With Addresses at Annual Meetings, Miscellaneous Papers, and a Roster of Kansas for Fifty Years.* Topeka, KS: George A. Clark, State Printer, 1904.

Martin, Michelle. "Mahala Doyle." *Kansas Journal of Military History* 1, no. 1 (Spring 2005): 31.

Meerse, David E. "The 1857 Territorial Delegate Election Contest." *Kansas History* 4, no. 2 (Summer 1981).

Mildfelt, Todd. *The Secret Danites: Kansas' First Jayhawkers.* Richmond, KS: Todd Mildfelt Publishing, 2003.

Miner, Craig. "Historic Ground: The Ongoing Enterprise of Kansas Territorial History." *Kansas History* 27, no. 1–2 (Spring–Summer 2004): 4.

———. *Kansas: The History of the Sunflower State, 1854–2000.* Lawrence: University Press of Kansas, 2002.

Monhollan, Rusty, and Kristen Tegtmeier Oertel. "From Brown to Brown: A Century of Struggle for Equality in Kansas." *Kansas History* 27, no. 1–2 (Spring–Summer 2004): 116.

Mullis, Tony R. "The Dispersal of the Topeka Legislature: A Look at Command and Control (C2) During Bleeding Kansas." *Kansas History* 27, no. 1–2 (Spring–Summer 2004): 62.

Napier, Rita G. "The Hidden History of Bleeding Kansas: Leavenworth and the Formation of the Free-State Movement." *Kansas History* 27, no. 1–2 (Spring–Summer 2004): 44.

Neely, Jeremy. *The Border Between Them: Violence and Reconciliation on the Kansas-Missouri Line.* Columbia: University of Missouri Press, 2007.

Pantle, Alberta. "The Connecticut Kansas Colony Letters of Charles B. Lines to the New Haven (Conn.) Daily Palladium." *Kansas Historical Quarterly* 22, no. 1 (Spring 1956) 1.

Peterson, John M., ed. "Letters of Edward and Sarah Fitch, Lawrence, Kansas, 1855–1863, Part II." *Kansas History* 12 (Summer 1989): 78–100.

Ponce, Pearl T. "Pledges and Principles: Buchannan Walker, and Kansas in 1857." *Kansas History* 27, no. 1–2 (Spring–Summer 2004): 86.

Prentis, Noble L. *A History of Kansas.* Topeka, KS: Caroline E. Prentis, 1904.

Price, Scott. *Nathaniel Lyon: Harbinger From Kansas.* Springfield, MO: Wilson's Creek National Battlefield Foundation, 1990.

Randall, Ruth Painter. *Mary Lincoln: Biography of a Marriage.* Boston: Little, Brown and Company, 1953.

Report of the Special Committee Appointed to Investigate the Troubles in Kansas; with the Views of the Minority of Said Committee. House Report No. 200, 34th Cong., 1st Sess. Washington, D.C.: Cornelius Wendell, printer, 1856, 1,193–99. Online at http://www.wvculture.org/history/jbexhibit/housecommittee.html.

Rich, Everett. *Heritage of Kansas.* Lawrence: University of Kansas Press, 1960.

Rosa, Joseph G., and Robin May. *Buffalo Bill and His Wild West.* Lawrence: University Press of Kansas, 1989.

Russell, Don, ed. "Julia Coty Goodman's Memoirs of Buffalo Bill." *Kansas Historical Quarterly* 28, no. 4 (Winter 1962): 442.

Rutherford, Phillip R. "The *Arabia* Incident." *Kansas History* 1, no. 1 (Spring 1978): 39.

Savage, Joseph. "Recollections of 1854." Territorial Kansas Online. www.territorialkansasonline.com.

SenGupta, Gunja. "Bleeding Kansas." *Kansas History* 24, no. 4 (Winter 2001–2002): 318.

Shortridge, James R. "People of the New Frontier: Kansas Population Origins, 1865." *Kansas History* 14, no. 3 (Autumn 1991): 162.

Smith, Ronald D. *Thomas Ewing Jr.: Frontier Lawyer and Civil War General.* Columbia: University of Missouri Press, 2008.

Socolofsky, Homer E., and Huber Self. *Historical Atlas of Kansas.* Norman: University of Oklahoma Press, 1972.

Stalnaker, Jeffrey D. *The Battle of Mine Creek: The Crushing End of the Missouri Campaign.* Charleston, SC: The History Press, 2011.

Tibbetts, John C. "Riding with the Devil: The Movie Adventures of William Clarke Quantrill." *Kansas History* 22, no. 3 (Autumn 1992): 182.

Treadway, William E. *Cyrus K. Holliday: A Documentary Biography.* Topeka, KS: Mainline Printing, Inc., 1979.

Wagnon, William O. "Wrecking Slavery from the Kansas Territory: The 'Topeka Boys' as Saboteurs, 1855–1861." Speech delivered at Omaha, Nebraska, March 4, 2005. Transcription with Shawnee County Historical Society, Topeka, Kansas.

Wallace, Douglass, ed. *The Capital's Storied Capitols: 1856–1886.* Topeka, KS: Shawnee County Historical Society, 2011.

Waskie, Anthony. *Philadelphia and the Civil War: Arsenal of the Union.* Charleston, SC: The History Press, 2011.

Westport Historical Society, ed. *The Battle of Westport.* 3rd ed. Kansas City, MO: self-published, 1996.

Wilder, D.W. *The Annals of Kansas 1541–1885.* Online at www.territorialkansasonline.org.

Williams, Burton J. "Quantrill's Raid on Lawrence: A Question of Complicity." *Kansas Historical Quarterly* 34, no. 2 (Summer 1968): 143.

Younger, Cole. *The Story of Cole Younger.* N.p.: self-published, 1903. Reprint, Triton Press, 1988.

Index

About the Author

A native Virginian, Deb has adopted Kansas as her home. She received her BA in history at Washburn University, Topeka, Kansas, and also studied at the Buffalo Bill Historical Center in Cody, Wyoming. Bleeding Kansas, the Civil War and the Plains Indian Wars are her areas of focus. She consults at the Command and General Staff College, Fort Leavenworth, on media training. History is Deb's first passion, and she has appeared in more than a dozen documentaries including, A&E's *American Experience* and productions for the History Channel, the Discovery Channel and PBS, and she has been a featured speaker on C-SPAN. Deb has been the guest on dozens of talk radio shows around the country, including Captain Dale Dye in Los Angeles and Jan Mickelson in Des Moines. Deb was the host of her own radio show, *Topeka Talks*, on KMAJ AM in Topeka. As a freelance journalist, she contributes regularly to *TK Magazine* and localgrass.com. She is active in many groups and is president of the Shawnee County Historical Society and co-president of the Civil War Roundtable of Eastern Kansas. She is married to musician Gary Bisel.

Deb Goodrich Bisel holds a remnant of the first flag to honor Kansas statehood, raised by president-elect Abraham Lincoln on February, 22, 1861, in front of Independence Hall. The artifact is owned by the Grand Army of the Republic Museum and Library in Philadelphia. *Photo by Gary Bisel.*